P9-DGZ-496

Chag sameach from Oorah to you
We hope you'll enjoy this gift, through and through.

Immerse yourself in it, enjoy, take a look
Get inspired, as you read from this book.

Enjoy the Chag throughout every stage
With the lessons you'll learn and gain from each page

And while you read, you'll know Oorah's near
Wherever you are, we're always here!

from
Rabbi Chaim Mintz

This book was donated in loving memory of
Dovid Winiarz z"l דוד אברהם בן חייא קהת ז"ל
by the Winiarz family

732-730-1000

www.oorah.org

REWARD MILES TO HEAVEN

BY

RABBI SHLOMO SCHWARTZ

Reward Miles to Heaven—
How to instantly upgrade the mitzvos you do
© 2007 by Rabbi Shlomo Schwartz

All rights reserved. No part of this publication may be translated, reproduced, stored in a retrieval system, or transmitted in any form or by any means, electronic, mechanical, photocopying, recording or otherwise, without permission in writing from the publisher.

ISBN: 978-1-932443-61-5

Editor: Diana Spechler
Proofreaders: Hadassa Goldsmith, Moshe Ibsen

THE JUDAICA PRESS, INC.
123 Ditmas Avenue / Brooklyn, NY 11218
718-972-6200 / 800-972-6201
info@judaicapress.com
www.judaicapress.com

Manufactured in the United States of America

aish
International

FOUNDER & DEAN
Rabbi Noah Weinberg

DAN FAMILY OF CANADA
WORLD CENTER
Jerusalem, Israel

AISH PROGRAMS
Aish.com
Aishaudio.com
Aish on Campus
Aish Productions
Discovery Production
EYAHT
Essentials
Executive Learning Center
Hasbara Fellowships
HonestReporting
Jerusalem Fellowships
Jerusalem Partners
JEWEL
Jewish Family Institute
Project Chazon
Russian Program
SpeedDating®
Spanish Division
The Jerusalem Fund
Yeshivat Aish HaTorah

AISH BRANCHES
Ashdod, Israel
Baltimore
Bat Yam, Israel
Birmingham, UK
Boston
Cleveland
Denver
Detroit
Essex, UK
Jerusalem, Israel
Johannesburg, SA
Kiev, Ukraine
Las Vegas
Livingston, NJ
London
Los Angeles
Manchester, UK
Melbourne, Australia
New York
Petach Tikva, Israel
Philadelphia
Santiago, Chile
Sao Paulo, Brazil
Scottsdale, AZ
Seattle
South Florida
St. Louis
Toronto
Washington, DC
Winnipeg, CA

Jerusalem
June 26, 2006

Rabbi Shloime Schwartz has done a wonderful job in helping us upgrade the performance of the mitzvoth that he discusses.
His thoughts are interesting and easy to read. I have not been able to read all of *Reward Miles To Heaven*, but the sections I have seen are clear in content and very useful.
Read, enjoy, and use.

Noah Weinberg

Rabbi Noah Weinberg
Founder and Rosh Yeshiva, Aish HaTorah

American Friends of Yeshiva Aish HaTorah, Inc.
400 South Lake Drive • Lakewood, NJ 08701-3167 • Tel: 732-364-6683 • Fax: 732-875-0576 • Email: info@aish.com
Tax ID# (EIN): 51-0243498 • Exemption granted pursuant to section 501(c)(3) of the Internal Revenue Code

YESHIVA SHAAREI MEIR

ישיבה וכולל שערי מאיר

הרב יעקב פרידמן
ראש הישיבה

בס"ד

לכבוד ידידי החשוב הר"ר שלמה שווארץ שליט"א
אביו של תלמידנו החשוב ומייסדי ישיבתנו הה"ר ישראל נ"י, היקר
והאהוב לנו עד למאוד

אחדשה"ט ונשה"ט.

קבלתי עלים לקראת מספרך החשוב. ונהניתי מאוד מדבריך היקרים. רואה שאתה קולמוס נפלא במלאכה זו לברר ולהבהיר מה שעובר בידינו הרבה מצוות בלי משים והבהרת בטוב טעם ודעת, ובפשטות, הדרך והאופן המכוון של כוונה בכל דבר ודבר. ואין ברורה היטב איך שאפשר להוסיף להרחיב ולהעמיק הרבה בדברים אלו שהן רק אנו עוסקים בהם תמיד, שאין בהם מצוות שבין אדם למקום ובין אדם לחבירו. ובידינו במעט שימת לב, לתקן ולכוון מעשינו ודרכינו - דרך הלוך חיינו הרגילים. שיהיו באמת שלמים כרצון שמים גדל ביופי המצוות ודקדוקיהן, היקר מאד ועיקר זה. (וע' בספר אהבת חסד פרק ד' אות ג' בהגה"ה ד"ה ועי').

כבודך הנחמדים והיקרים שנכתבו בלשון צח וברור בחכמה ודייקנות, ועריכת המצוות האלו לבנינו בקלות וברור. בסדר נפלא ובאופן המעורר עניין באמת. יישר כחך! ויה"ר שמלאכתו מלאכה שיפוצו מעינותיך חוצה מתוך שפע ברכה, והרחבת הדעת, ומתוך נחת רוח מכל יוצאי חלציך ובריאות השלמים, וכט"ס.

ידידך המוקירך
יעקב פרידמן

Mailing Address:
Israel: Nachal Nachshon 3/12 P.O. Box 60664 Ramat Beit Shemesh, ISRAEL
USA: "Friends of Yeshiva Shaarei Meir", 15 Herschel Terrace, Monsey, NY 10952

DEDICATION

To my mother, Blanche Schwartz
—a.k.a. "Aunty Blanche" to the rest of the world—
who always admonished,
"Remember who you are and where you come from."

And to my father-in-law, Mordechai Bressler
—a.k.a. "MB" to everyone else—
who remembered vividly and kept it alive.

"Biz hindred und tzvantzik!"
May they continue to enjoy the fruits of their efforts.

ACKNOWLEDGMENTS

The publication of my first book is the realization of a lifelong goal and I feel I must acknowledge all those who led me and helped me reach this point. As I think back, I can see now that Hashem's hand has guided me every step of the way.

At the age of nine, I was blessed to have been one of the first students of Rabbi Akiva Greenberg, a legendary teacher for over fifty years now. I suspect that my deep gratification in teaching others comes from trying to replicate his great joy and enthusiasm for Yiddishkeit. And I would never have met Rabbi Greenberg had it not been for my Zaidie, Chaim Yosef Orzech, *a"h*, who conducted an early version of a sit-in to get me enrolled in the Eitz Chaim day school, and for my Uncle Yosef Mandel who, with an amazing combination of determination and insight, harangued the administration to transfer me to Rabbi Greenberg's class.

My first mentor upon entering Ner Israel Yeshiva College of Toronto was Avraham Zelig Safransky, *z"l*. He taught mostly by example and his demise at an early age was a great loss to the Torah world. In those early years at Ner Israel, I was blessed with exceptional Rebbeim and mentors, as evidenced by their future accomplishments and reputations. In the order that I met them, they were: Rabbi Sholom Gold, Rabbi Pinchas Lipner, Rabbi Chaim Mintz, Rabbi Gershon Weiss, Rabbi Nota Schiller, Rabbi

Noach Weinberg, Rabbi Reuven Silver, Rabbi Yochanan Zweig, Rabbi Uziel Milevsky, *z"l,* and Rabbi Moshe Hochman.

Despite all the gifts that Hashem has given me, I still would never have accomplished what little I have had Hashem not then arranged for me to study under Rav Yaakov Weinberg, *zt"l,* who, over the course of five years, taught me how to learn Torah. I cannot begin to assess my debt to him.

More recently, in specific regard to this book, I want to thank those stalwarts who stayed with me as I developed this material, day after day, after Shacharis at Aish HaTorah Thornhill. They were: Joe Berman, *a"h,* Alan Kleiman, Mordechai Prokopets, *a"h*, Reuven Saul and Fred Silver. I am also very grateful for the learned advice I received from Rav Meir Stern of Passaic and Rav Moshe Goldberger of Staten Island.

I also wish to mention two people who are unaware of their involvement. They are: Rabbi Ben Zion Sobel, whose preface to *The Concise Book of Mitzvoth* (Feldheim, 1990) inspired the development of the "reward miles" concept, and Rabbi Zelig Pliskin, whose upbeat writing style provided a template for this work.

Once the manuscript was accepted, Nachum Shapiro of Judaica Press kept me on track and Diana Spechler, my editor, did a marvelous job of encouraging me on even as she shredded my syntax and highlighted my obtuseness. This book is vastly improved because of them.

Last but not least, I would like to thank my wife Shaynie—but I don't know how. It's like trying to appreciate your right hand; where do you draw the line between yourself and your right hand? So let's just say that I wrote this book, and she wrote a good part of me. She can take the credit. I will take the responsibility.

CONTENTS

"Remember this important
principle when doing mitzvos—
it all depends on the intent
of your heart, as Chazal said,
'*Rachmana liba ba'i*—
G-d desires the heart'
(*Sanhedrin* 106b).
Accordingly ... a single mitzvah
performed with the proper
intent is worth more than
a multitude of mitzvos
done without."

—*Sefer HaIkarim*, ch. 27

READ ME

Many of the commonplace things that we do every day have tremendous spiritual potential, because they are actually mitzvos. If we would stop for just a second to consider that when we do these seemingly mundane tasks we are actually fulfilling the wishes of the Creator of the universe, we would realize enormous spiritual dividends.

This thought is really just a corollary of the halacha that *"mitzvos tzrichos kavana,"* mitzvos require intent (see *Mishnah Berurah* 60:4), about which the Chofetz Chaim reportedly remarked: "How pitiful it is that we lose so many *mitzvos d'Oraisa* because we lack intent."

This book aims to help us discover the proper motivation and get our *full* reward. In thirty brief lessons, it identifies the true—and sometimes surprising—definitions of many mitzvos and reveals how many of our routine activities actually encompass these mitzvos. Armed with this knowledge, we can infuse our actions throughout the day with the proper intent. The effect of this simple change can be astounding. It can enliven and uplift our life in this world, and dramatically upgrade our share in the World to Come.

Reward Miles to Heaven

The airline reward miles concept offers an excellent analogy. When we purchase airline tickets or other items, we're buying things we would buy anyway. But if we make the purchase with our air miles card, we earn a valuable bonus—airline tickets—for free. *All we have to do is remember to use our card.*

The same is true with mitzvos. When we give someone a car ride, when we help carry in the groceries, when we offer someone constructive criticism, *we're doing these things anyway.* But if we have in mind when we do them that we're fulfilling a mitzvah, and even more so when we know exactly which mitzvah we're doing, we earn valuable bonuses for free—our life in this world becomes much more meaningful, and we'll earn a vastly greater reward in the World to Come.

All we have to add is our awareness.

TELL ME MORE!

It Only Makes Sense

It only makes sense that a mitzvah should require intent. After all, the purpose of fulfilling mitzvos is to build a relationship with the Almighty. Every relationship is based on both parties' behaving, *consciously*, according to the desires of the other. No one is impressed with the person who opens the door in front of him only if he is walking through anyway; the person who succeeds in a relationship is the one who opens the door specifically for the other person, putting the other person's desires in front of his own.

The mitzvos are the Almighty's desires. To build a relationship with Him, one must fulfill His desires on purpose, not by accident. As the Mishnah says in *Pirkei Avos* (2:4), "Make your will His so that He will make His will yours." That is a relationship.

A relationship with G-d is possible even when the relationship is self-serving. Indeed, most relationships begin because they are rewarding. This doesn't necessarily conflict with the Mishnah in *Pirkei Avos* (1:3), which warns against being like a servant who serves his master for the sake of the reward. It is not a sin to serve for the sake of the reward. Serving without expectation of reward is simply more exalted; it is an elevated state that not everyone reaches. Many people work harder if they can anticipate a reward; those people should absolutely keep the reward in sight. They are all the more justified when the anticipated reward is as great as the reward for doing mitzvos promises to be; according to another Mishnah in *Pirkei Avos* (4:22), one moment of spiritual bliss in the World to Come is more pleasurable than all the pleasures of this world.

Still Not Sure About the Program?

With such a reward at stake, everyone should be highly motivated to perform each mitzvah properly, especially if all that is missing from the mitzvah is the conscious intent. After all, if someone is already doing the mitzvah, why not take that extra step to make it count more? As logical as this may seem, some people have trouble mustering enthusiasm because they cannot comprehend the reward. If I promised someone a billion dollars for shining my shoes, for example, he might be skeptical, even if I proved that I was serious. A billion dollars is just too good to be true! For people who cannot comprehend the rewards of the World to Come, it might help to contemplate the more immediate, and therefore more believable, benefits of performing mitzvos consciously.

The awareness of being engaged in a mitzvah makes the mitzvah-doer's actions more meaningful; after all, what could be more meaningful than performing exactly as the Creator intended? The conscious mitzvah-doer will perform the mitzvah with greater dignity, energy and conviction, and will in turn feel a deep sense of confidence, serenity and ultimate joy. These benefits are more tangible than the benefits in the World to Come, and are therefore easier to strive for.

It is extremely difficult for us to change our behavior. For proof, just consider the diet and self-help industry, which cashes in on people's proven tendency to fail. However, I am addressing behavior that is already a part of us. My objective is simply to point out activities that we are already doing that can qualify as mitzvos. From there, all we need is a flash of awareness that we are doing that particular mitzvah. It's as effortless as flashing a reward miles card at the time of purchase. That flash transforms the action and leads to Heavenly reward!

A Proper Frame of Mind

"**M**itzvah" has been traditionally translated as "commandment," but that may no longer be the best translation. Modern times are an age of unprecedented personal freedom, the likes of which would have been unimaginable to the great-grandparents of today's generation, and every generation before them. For those bygone generations, rules and commandments were normal and expected. For people today, commandments chafe; no one likes to be ordered around. However, people today do appreciate guidance. Who hasn't heard, "Just tell me what I have to do," from the frustrated teenager, the new man on the job or the beleaguered spouse?

Therefore, if the word "commandment" seems too harsh, we can choose to view a "mitzvah" as an "instruction" (albeit an obligatory one). Rav Noach Weinberg, founder and Rosh Yeshiva of Aish HaTorah, inspired this interpretation by explaining that "*Toras Chaim*," another term for "Torah," means "instructions for living." He explains that if a person gave someone a car as a gift, the recipient would undoubtedly be extremely grateful. Until the car's brakes failed. Then the recipient might come screaming to the gift-giver that the gift had almost killed him.

"Did you service the brakes?" the gift-giver might ask.

"No," the recipient would answer. "How was I supposed to know to do that?"

"It's in the manual," the gift-giver would reply. "Didn't you read the manual that came with the car?"

Now, if the gift had been a jumbo airplane, it, too, would have come with a manual, and, because a jumbo airplane can do so much more than a car, that manual would probably comprise a small library. Since the Creator has given people the greatest gift, the gift of life, it only makes sense that life should come with a manual. That manual is the Torah, and the mitzvos are the instructions for how to make the most out of life.

By constantly referring to mitzvos as instructions, I hope to make it easier for the reader to remember when he is performing a mitzvah activity and to anticipate the spiritual benefits that might accrue from following that instruction.

Where Did I Get This From?

The primary sources that I relied on for the mitzvos and their meanings were the Torah, the *Sefer HaMitzvos HaKatzar* by the Chofetz Chaim, and the *Sefer HaChinuch*. (The *Sefer HaChinuch* was written in the Middle Ages as an overview of all the mitzvos, following the order in which they appear in the Torah. Its author is known as "the *Chinuch*.") I started with the original texts in Hebrew, but usually double-checked with the English versions. I find that it's important to study a text both in its original language and in a translation in my native tongue in order to ensure complete integration of the material. Unfortunately, it is not uncommon to learn something in the original Hebrew and promptly, albeit unintentionally, dismiss it as abstract. Without verbalizing the concept in the language with which we conduct our daily life, we sometimes fail to see the information as personally relevant.

In fact, this very problem inspired me to write this book: I had learned the relevant chapters in the *Shulchan Aruch* and *Mishnah Berurah* about "*mitzvos tzrichos kavana*" a few times. However, the ramifications eluded me until I saw the same idea written in my native tongue in Ben Zion Sobel's preface to *The Concise Book of Mitzvoth* (the English edition of the *Sefer HaMitzvos HaKatzar*). True, the wisdom of advanced years probably also helped me recognize the broader impact of what I was reading. Nevertheless, I find that whenever I am able to consult an English translation after reading the original Hebrew, I gain new insights into the material. For this reason, I urge the reader to do the same.

How This Book Is Structured

I have selected for discussion only a portion of those mitzvah instructions that we are already performing. With the hope of introducing mitzvah awareness into our lives one area at a time, I have grouped the selected mitzvos under the following headings:

- **The Golden Rules**
- **Maintain Your Orbit**
- **Get a Life, Give a Life**
- **It's Just Good Business**

Within each mitzvah, I have divided the presentation into several sections:

› **The Basic Instruction**—presents a verse from the Torah, identifies the mitzvah derived from it and cites references to the corresponding sections in the Chofetz Chaim's *The Concise Book of Mitzvoth* and in the *Sefer HaChinuch*, respectively, so that the reader can easily look up the source.

› **Let's Discuss**—discusses some salient features of each mitzvah, particularly those features mentioned by either the Chofetz Chaim or the *Chinuch*. These discussions are by no means thorough renderings of the scope of each mitzvah. Rather, I hope that these sections will uncover those features of each mitzvah that influence current, conventional behavior.

› **We Do This All the Time**, or, in the case of a prohibition,
› **We Often Avoid This**—identifies specific examples of common behavior that conform to the mitzvah in that section, and that would become more rewarding in many ways if the mitzvah-doer simply infused the act with awareness. The goal of these sections is to enhance common behavior with a mitzvah-consciousness.

› **We Can Do Even Better**—for some mitzvos, the heightened awareness leads naturally to opportunities for improved behavior, so I offer suggestions on how we can go beyond our routine behavior.

› **Put It Into Action**—this section summarizes and lists some of the many opportunities we have to put our newfound mitzvah consciousness into action.

› **Notes and Observations**—a place for you to record your own personal practices (existing or intended) that could benefit from this heightened awareness.

THE GOLDEN RULES

To start collecting reward miles, let's start with everyone's favorite, the Golden Rule: "Love your neighbor as yourself." This rule is not what most people imagine it to be, so it provides ample opportunity for enhanced understanding and consciousness. It is noteworthy that the Torah presents us with a number of related mitzvos, grouped together in just a few verses, implying that not just one, but quite a few, Golden Rules exist.

וְאָהַבְתָּ לְרֵעֲךָ כָּמוֹךָ

"You shall love your neighbor as yourself" (Lev. 19:18)

Love Your Neighbor

The Basic Instruction

The Torah states, "You shall not avenge nor bear any grudge against the children of your people, rather you shall love your neighbor as yourself" (Lev. 19:18). From the latter half of the verse, the reader derives the mitzvah to love his neighbor as himself. In a nutshell, this mitzvah instructs the reader to maintain the same protective concern for another person's safety, health, assets and self-esteem that he has for his own. The Chofetz Chaim presents this as the 60th positive instruction in *The Concise Book of Mitzvoth*, and the *Chinuch* discusses it under mitzvah number 243.

"Love your neighbor as yourself" is a world-famous mitzvah. Even among many non-Jews, it is known as the Golden Rule. Many societies have some version of it. For this, we should thank G-d, because the alternative, "every man for himself," would be a societal disaster.

Even though most people are familiar with this mitzvah, it is worthwhile to examine its full scope. By learning more about the mitzvah, we can identify instances when we regularly perform it, and then learn to do so with conscious intent. The full scope of the mitzvah emanates from three interpretations, which, though different, do not necessarily contradict each other.

Let's Discuss Interpretation #1:

The Common Understanding

The first and most common understanding of the mitzvah is to be kind and courteous. Every day during the morning service, we recite a Talmudic dictum (*Shabbos* 127a) that lists some prominent methods of being kind and courteous. The methods include welcoming guests, visiting the sick, providing for the bride (through gifts and merry-making at the wedding), attending to the burial of the dead and forging peace between two people.

We Do This All the Time!

It is true that people are frequently kind and courteous, but often, people act that way out of habit or personal interest. People are kind and courteous because they are raised to be kind and courteous. Kindness and courtesy are as natural for them as wearing clothes. They welcome guests and visit the sick because the guests and the patients are their friends, and they feel genuine concern for them. People make merry at weddings because weddings are, indeed, joyous occasions. And so on. These are all excellent reasons for acting kind and courteous. However, while it is important to internalize the lessons of the Torah so that they naturally infuse our behavior, it is even better to be aware of the mitzvah aspect of the behavior. Doing so will help us internalize our relationship with the Almighty and gain a sublime intimacy with Him. Keep it in mind!

Let's Discuss Interpretation #2: The Real Thing

The next aspect of the mitzvah, "Love your neighbor as yourself," appears to be a subset of the foregoing aspect, but actually, it replaces that aspect with a concept that has a sharper focus and a greater intensity. This new aspect emerges from a careful reading of the sources.

The Chofetz Chaim explains that the way to perform the "Love your neighbor" mitzvah is to give the same care and concern to the health, property and dignity of fellow Jews that we give ourselves. Such care includes the act of fostering peace and harmony between two Jews. The *Chinuch* concurs, as does the Rambam in *Mishneh Torah*. The most remarkable distinction these Sages make is that the mitzvah applies exclusively to the behavior of one Jew to another. Apparently, the Sages all translate the Hebrew word "*rey'acha*" ("neighbor" or "fellow") to mean "Jew." In other words, the mitzvah, "Love your fellow as yourself," continues to encourage all of the kindnesses and courtesies described above, but only when practiced among fellow Jews.

This distinction is problematic because it makes us vulnerable to attack from people all over the world who can (and do) accuse the Jewish people of plotting against them. Because no one can change the teachings of our Sages, who have meticulously preserved the true meanings of the Torah, we must seek a satisfactory explanation for this exclusivity within the context that the Sages have provided.

Of course, Jewish history and Torah culture contradict the notion that the Jewish people denigrate or seek to take advantage of non-Jews. Torah prohibitions against murder, robbery, infidelity, injury and oppression apply universally. More importantly, Jews generally do practice kindness and courtesy to everyone, to Jews and non-Jews alike. Someone once told me that my rebbi,

Rav Yaakov Weinberg, *zt"l*, said that the Jewish tendency toward universal kindness comes from the mitzvah to model ourselves after the Almighty, to be like G-d. In the words of our Sages, just as He is merciful, so must we be; just as He is gracious, so must we be; and so on. Indeed, since the Almighty certainly loves every human (as is evidenced by each person's very existence and all of his or her human potential), so must we love every human. And so we do.

What, then, is the special significance of "Love your neighbor as yourself"? Why do we need this mitzvah when we already have the broader mitzvah to be like G-d? My rebbi, Rav Yaakov Weinberg, *zt"l*, taught that the answer lies in the phrase "as yourself." The mitzvah underscores the great affection that Jews must engender for each other. The Jewish people must see itself as one body, and therefore, treat each member as a part of its own body. Just as it would be foolish to cut off your nose to spite your face, it would be foolish for a Jew to harm a fellow Jew.

The Almighty has given the Jewish people the mission to bring peace and harmony to all mankind ("I will appoint thee for a light unto the nations so that My salvation may reach as far as the end of the earth," Isaiah 49:6). Just as no corporation can function if its staff does not work together as a team, only by maintaining concern for the health and welfare of each fellow Jew can the Jewish people unite to achieve their goal. Any attack on this unity is a very serious breach. Therefore, the Chofetz Chaim cites the Sages' declaration that one who derives honor from another Jew's disgrace forfeits his share in the World to Come.

We Do This All the Time!

We love our neighbors as ourselves all the time! The Jewish community is renowned for its many "*chesed*" institutions: homes for the aged, hospitals, burial societies, job placement bureaus, special schools, etc. And Jews are kind for the right reason: a sense of obligation to help one another. Still, to perform the mitzvah even better, and to enjoy it more (especially when faced with difficult "clients"), we must remember that we are fulfilling the will of the Almighty.

We also regularly engage in the "Love your neighbor" mitzvah in minor ways (that is, minor in terms of effort, but no less important in terms of the mitzvah). Giving directions, lending articles, offering a lift, sharing financial advice or shopping advice, saying "Excuse me" and holding the door open are some of the thousands of little kindnesses, and therefore, mitzvos, that people perform out of friendship or courtesy. Remembering the mitzvah and its great reward, and being consciously engaged in binding the Jewish people together, infuses each act of kindness with more meaning and purpose.

We Can Do Even Better

The main goal of this book is to highlight opportunities for earning great reward without exerting extra effort beyond cultivating a higher level of awareness. A secondary goal is to highlight instances in which a greater awareness might inspire greater effort. Two such instances follow.

Perhaps the place where we most need to inject conscious intent is into our own homes. The home is the most opportune venue for us to treat others the way we treat ourselves. For example, most of us appreciate being able to find things; therefore, we could put things back after using them so that others will be able to find them. Also, because most of us do not like our own sleep disturbed, we should be quiet when others have retired to bed earlier.

However, we may often feel that we are treating our family members better than we treat ourselves, which leads to resentment. The "Love your neighbor" mitzvah can help soften that attitude. We may still feel the sting of resentment, but the proper awareness provides a balm for the sting.

Shopping is another opportunity to let better awareness lead to greater effort. Often, small shopkeepers, members of the community, sell the products that chain stores sell, but for a higher price. While the small shopkeeper may offer other benefits, such as closer proximity, more personalized service or delivery, the shopper might not need those benefits and might ask himself why he should pay more than necessary. The answer lies in this mitzvah: We must express the same concern for a fellow Jew's livelihood that we would for our own.

Let's Discuss Interpretation #3: The Famous Saying

Rabbi Akiva encapsulates the third interpretation of the mitzvah in his famous comment on it: "This is a significant summarization of the Torah." The *Chinuch* explains Rabbi Akiva's interpretation to mean that loving your neighbor prevents you from transgressing many of the Torah's prohibitions, such as those against theft, adultery, oppression, inflicting injury and disadvantaging others' businesses. In this way, "Love your neighbor as yourself" stands as the positive counterpart to a number of Torah prohibitions.

The *Chinuch*'s interpretation of Rabbi Akiva's words seems to suggest that restraint from violating a prohibition, such as "Do not take revenge," is, at the same time, an affirmative adherence to the mitzvah of loving your neighbor. That is, two mitzvos are accomplished at the same time when we refrain from taking revenge. Normally, a person's conscious awareness of the evil of taking revenge is what deters him from doing so; such restraint would earn the full mitzvah reward. The *Chinuch* teaches that a person can gain extra reward by being conscious of the mitzvah, "Love your neighbor," whenever he refrains from violating one of its counterpart prohibitions.

We Do This All the Time!

We are often tempted to inflict harm on others, but we refrain for a variety of reasons. One reason might be the Torah instruction that inflicting harm is wrong. At the moment we refrain from inflicting harm on someone, we can use the experience to enhance and develop our feelings of concern for that person (an expression of love for our neighbor). This consciousness will establish a positive connection with the other person. Once we are able to connect with someone we wished to harm, then, by extension, we should be able to connect more easily with everyone else. Here is a chance for all of us to feel positive about ourselves and our place in the world. We should keep it in mind!

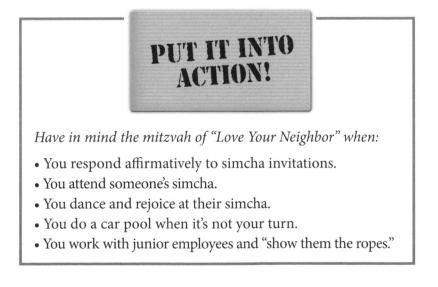

PUT IT INTO ACTION!

Have in mind the mitzvah of "Love Your Neighbor" when:

- You respond affirmatively to simcha invitations.
- You attend someone's simcha.
- You dance and rejoice at their simcha.
- You do a car pool when it's not your turn.
- You work with junior employees and "show them the ropes."

- You deliberately patronize Jewish shops instead of getting a better deal at a national chain store.
- You buy and/or give someone a present.
- You share your solutions to common challenges (e.g., household management, child rearing, etc.) with family, friends or acquaintances.
- You volunteer for a community organization (e.g., health care facility, school, chessed project, etc.).
- You make a call to cheer up a friend who's feeling down.
- You act courteously, listen to others, or simply offer a friendly smile to people you greet.

Notes and Observations

לֹא־תִקֹּם ... אֶת־בְּנֵי עַמֶּךָ

"You shall not take revenge ... against your people"
(Lev. 19:18)

Do Not Take Revenge

The Basic Instruction

As previously noted, only the latter half of the verse instructs people to love their neighbor as themselves. The first part of the verse, "You shall not avenge nor bear any grudge against the children of your people" (Lev. 19:18), warns against taking revenge. It makes sense that the Torah would introduce these two mitzvos in the same verse because they express a common theme, namely, improving interpersonal relations. Nevertheless, the details governing the two mitzvos are different. The Chofetz Chaim presents the "revenge" mitzvah as the 80th in his list of negatives, while the *Chinuch* discusses it under mitzvah number 241.

Let's Discuss

The Chofetz Chaim explains the nature of revenge with this classic example: Person A asks to borrow a tool from Person B, but Person B refuses Person A. Later, when Person B wants to borrow something from Person A, Person A refuses him, saying, "I will not lend it to you, since you refused to lend to me." This is the classic act of revenge.

The *Chinuch* seems to define this prohibition somewhat

differently, and his approach is more understandable within the context of the ensuing, related prohibition: the instruction not to bear a grudge. Accordingly, the following discussion is based solely on the Chofetz Chaim's definition of the mitzvah.

We Often Avoid This

It is not uncommon for a person to feel let down by his friends. Sometimes, even strangers, by eschewing common courtesies, can leave people feeling betrayed. In such situations, it is only natural to feel resentful, or worse, to want to repay the guilty party in kind. Nevertheless, people push such thoughts aside for any number of reasons: They might feel it is beneath them to stoop to that level, confrontation might escalate to a situation beyond their control, or the revenge simply wouldn't be worth the time and effort.

Feelings of resentment and desires to seek revenge are opportunities to perform the mitzvah not to seek revenge! One cannot fulfill a negative mitzvah when either the motivation or the opportunity to violate the mitzvah is absent. For example, I cannot claim credit for having fulfilled the prohibition against murder while I slept or was alone on a desert island because I had no opportunity to commit murder under such circumstances. Similarly, I cannot claim credit for having avoided murdering my friends while socializing with them because I had no motivation to murder them.

A negative mitzvah can only be considered fulfilled when both motivation and opportunity exist and are overcome by a conscious desire to adhere to the mitzvah. Although other factors prevent people from seeking revenge, only a conscious desire to adhere to the mitzvah constitutes fulfillment of the mitzvah. Such awareness leads to consciousness of the Almighty's will and provides the mitzvah-doer an intimate connection with Him.

Keeping the mitzvah in mind will also strengthen our resolve to avoid seeking revenge for the other reasons (not stooping to such low behavior, not wanting to escalate the issue and not wasting energy on trivialities). After all, these factors are undoubtedly some of the Almighty's reasons for giving us the mitzvah not to take revenge.

MITZVOS TO DO *and* NOT TO DO

Categorizing mitzvos as either positive or negative comes from the Torah. Mitzvos framed as instructions for performing certain acts are called positives. Those framed as warnings against certain behaviors are called negatives. For example, "Love your neighbor" is a positive, while "Do not take revenge" is a negative.

It is not always clear why some mitzvos are expressed one way and not the other. For example, "Love your neighbor" has been recast by some sources as both "Do unto others as you would have them do unto you" and "Don't do unto others what you would not have them do unto you." (These phrasings and others are the subject of an interesting essay by Dr. J. H. Hertz, late chief Rabbi of the British Empire, presented as Additional Note D to Leviticus in the Pentateuch, Soncino Press, 1971, p. 563.)

Similarly, the mitzvah that forbids revenge could have theoretically been expressed as a positive instruction. For example, the colloquialism "fugeddaboudit" (another way of saying, "forget about it") could provide a positive alternative to the prohibition against revenge (i.e., "Forget about taking revenge"). So why is this mitzvah phrased as a negative?

To explain, I suggest thinking of the mitzvos as instructions from a parent: A parent instructs his child to participate in activities that will benefit the child's welfare, and to avoid activities and behaviors that could harm the child. Our Father in Heaven, who is lovingly concerned and powerfully involved in His people's welfare, does the same for His people. Support for this approach may be found in the comments of the Ramban (Nachmanides) on the Ten Commandments (Exod. 20:8), where he describes positive mitzvos as instances of G-d's love for us (conveying benefits), while negative mitzvos demonstrate our fear of punishment and awe of G-d (protecting us from harm).

Using this theory to contemplate the mitzvos might provide new insights about the mitzvos' meanings and value. For example, people can certainly learn things about themselves if, indeed, all the positive mitzvos describe behaviors that benefit people, and all the negative mitzvos describe behaviors that harm people.

Befriending neighbors cements a community and builds a support group that benefits every member. Not befriending neighbors does not destroy society; it just leaves it cold and impersonal. There is no harm, but no benefit, either. Therefore, the Torah gives the positive instruction to love your neighbor so that people can reap the benefits.

Although abstaining from revenge may not produce a benefit, it prevents further harm, whereas revenge does harm not only to the victim but (perhaps even more so) to the avenger. Even for those who claim that revenge is sweet, it is, apparently, never sweet enough because people often seek revenge that is worse or more frequent than the original crime. By proscribing revenge through a negative mitzvah, the Torah provides insight into how a person can become harmfully consumed by insatiable rage.

PUT IT INTO ACTION!

Have in mind the mitzvah of "Do Not Take Revenge" when:

- You feel resentment and the desire to seek revenge for a perceived wrong, and you choose to restrain yourself.

Notes and Observations

וְלֹא־תִטֹּר אֶת־בְּנֵי עַמֶּךָ

"You shall not ... bear any grudge against your people" (Lev. 19:18)

Do Not Bear a Grudge

The Basic Instruction

The Torah's instruction not to bear a grudge comes from the verse that also instructs, "You shall not avenge," and, "You shall love your neighbor as yourself." The relevant words are, "nor bear any grudge against your people" (Lev. 19:18). The Chofetz Chaim presents this as the 81st item in his list of negatives, and the *Chinuch* discusses it under mitzvah number 242.

Let's Discuss

What is bearing a grudge? The Chofetz Chaim defines it by continuing the classic example of revenge. Person B previously refused to loan Person A some item. Now, Person B asks Person A if he can borrow some item. Instead of taking revenge by responding, "I am refusing you, just like you refused me," Person A says, "I will lend it to you, even though you didn't lend to me." Person A is innocent of taking revenge, but guilty of bearing a grudge. However, it is not just the words, "I will lend it to you, even though you didn't lend to me," that imply a grudge. The crime is not in the words, but rather in the feeling of animosity that the words reveal.

To quote the *Chinuch*, "We are forbidden to keep in our heart any ill-feeling over the harm that any Jew did to us. Even if we should resolve not to repay him in kind for his deeds, the mere remembrance in the heart of his sin is forbidden to us."

The *Chinuch* expresses a similar ruling in regard to revenge: It is not revenge itself, but the attitude that yields the revenge, that is prohibited. Once someone has vowed to hate another person until revenge is exacted, even if he never gets his revenge, he has violated the mitzvah, "You shall not avenge."

This remarkable ruling reveals a profound insight into the Torah's teaching. The problem with revenge is not only the harm that one may inflict on the other person, but the harm the revenge-seeker inflicts on himself. The Torah reveals how self-destructive it is to harbor hatred in your heart and to bear a grudge is to do just that.

So when someone is wronged, what should he do with those natural feelings of animosity? According to the *Chinuch*, he must realize that any harm that befalls him must be ascribed to the Almighty. After all, He is in charge! G-d allows for harm, either to teach a person a lesson or to cleanse him from some fault. (Of course, the person inflicting harm cannot thereby justify his own actions; the Almighty has no shortage of means to carry out His will and did not need his help. He just made use of the wicked person's evil intention.)

When we experience personal harm, we should try to humbly remember the Almighty's role in that harm. Who can contend with the Almighty Creator of the Universe? Ironically, that very act of humility elevates and ennobles people. The *Chinuch* seeks to inspire this level of nobility by relating a story about King David, father of all rightful kings of Israel, and therefore Jewish history's quintessential model for nobility. The story is about Shimi ben Gera, who was overheard cursing King David. When David's followers found out, they wanted to punish Shimi severely. However, David stopped them with these words: "So let him curse, for G-d has told him to curse David" (Samuel II 16:10). In other words, David resigned himself to the insult because of his conviction that it had emanated from the Almighty.

We Often Avoid This

It may seem much too demanding, not to mention unnatural, for a person to completely erase ill feelings for those who have offended, injured or insulted him. And once we use the word "unnatural," we usually feel justified in bearing our "natural" grudges.

However, we should not be so quick to reject the goal of relinquishing grudges. People act "unnaturally" all the time, with great results. Civilization itself is predicated on the human ability to control natural desires. Employing table manners, for example, modifies and controls the natural desire to eat quickly and without consideration for others. After the appropriate training, people manage table manners effortlessly. By the same token, through training and practice, people can control the urge to retaliate.

People constantly perform the mitzvah of not bearing grudges with their children (not to mention with their spouses and close friends). Children often act in obnoxious and offensive ways, but, out of love, parents quickly forgive and forget their bad behavior; they do not wish to harbor antagonism toward their own children. Now look at the result!

Because parents forgive and forget, they continue to love and enjoy their children. If they expanded their willingness to forgive to other people, they could maintain peaceful relationships with everyone, not just with their children, and avoid creating new antagonists.

When we quickly resolve to forgive and forget, we should keep the mitzvah not to bear a grudge in mind for two reasons. First, being conscious of the mitzvah is an opportunity to gain reward miles to Heaven because we have performed a mitzvah, even if performing it was easy. Second, being conscious of the mitzvah will help us realize our ability to act forgiving, which may in turn encourage us to expand our capacity for forgiveness to include more people. Expanding our capacity to forgive will surely lead to immeasurable self-improvement. We can employ any number of behavior tricks to facilitate forgiveness, but conscious awareness is surely the start.

PUT IT INTO ACTION!

Have in mind the mitzvah of "Do Not Bear a Grudge" when:

- Things are hectic, and you choose to ignore slight offenses.
- A reckless driver turns out to be someone you know and you decide to put it out of your mind.
- You try to tolerate and adjust to someone's bad habit.
- You decide to ignore a work colleague's momentary loss of temper.

Notes and Observations

הוֹכֵחַ תּוֹכִיחַ אֶת־עֲמִיתֶךָ

"You shall surely rebuke your fellow"
(Lev. 19:17)

Speak Up and Speak Out, but Speak Softly

The Basic Instruction

The Torah states, "Do not hate your brother in your heart; you shall surely rebuke your fellow and not bear sin because of him" (Lev. 19:17). From the three clauses in this verse come three separate, yet closely related, mitzvos. From the positive mitzvah in the second clause, "you shall surely rebuke your fellow," comes the instruction to speak up to disapprove of a fellow Jew's bad behavior. The Chofetz Chaim presents this mitzvah as the 72nd item in his list of positives, and the *Chinuch* presents it under mitzvah number 239.

There are two types of bad behavior that people could criticize: sinful behavior and impolite behavior. By impolite behavior I mean behavior that may be annoying, rude or offensive, but cannot be termed an outright sin. Some examples might be a person who interrupts, who appears inconsiderate, who is always late, or who complains about everything. The Chofetz Chaim discusses impolite behavior in light of the mitzvah not to hate secretly (the first part of the verse), in contrast to both the *Chinuch* and the Rambam (Maimonides). In the *Mishneh Torah, Hilchos Deos*, chapter six, paragraph six, the Rambam seems to say that this positive mitzvah ("you shall surely rebuke your fellow") includes criticism of impolite behavior (see also *Sefer HaMitzvos*). For presentation purposes, I follow the lead of the Chofetz Chaim and limit my discussion of the mitzvah, "you shall surely rebuke your fellow," to sinful behavior.

Let's Discuss

The Rabbis emphasize that the primary goal when criticizing sinful behavior is to help the sinner. The person doing the criticizing should want to help the sinner, and thereby avoid unfavorable consequences, both here and in the World to Come. (Indeed, the very next verse in Leviticus instructs, "Love your neighbor as yourself.") Therefore, before communicating disapproval of sinful behavior, the person doing the criticizing must first impress the sinner with his desire and intent to help. He should criticize in private to avoid causing the sinner embarrassment, and he should speak in a conciliatory voice that conveys his concern and love.

The verse, "you shall surely rebuke," is one suggested translation of an idiomatic expression that literally reads, "you shall rebuke, rebuke." The Rabbis infer from this verse the instruction to rebuke more than once, as many times as necessary to get the "fellow" to change. A person who can positively influence another, but does not try to do so, assumes the guilt of the sin. Hence, the verse's finale: "and do not bear sin because of him."

If the admonishments are ignored, the admonisher is duty-bound to go so far as to embarrass the sinner publicly in hopes of changing the sinner's behavior. (This does not apply when the admonisher is the victim seeking retribution, but only to someone sincerely trying to help the sinner.) Just as a parent persists with every available tool in teaching a child as many skills as possible, and just as that parent is not dissuaded by the child's constant failures or by his refusal to cooperate, so should a person persist in helping his "fellow" to reform. Public embarrassment may also achieve a secondary goal: helping onlookers to resist following the sinner's bad example.

We may only desist from criticizing when we are sure, based on the sinner's reaction, that our criticisms are doing more harm than good. According to the Rabbis, just as it is a religious obligation to rebuke, so is it a religious obligation to be silent when it is clear that rebukes will go unheeded; otherwise, not only does the sinner not benefit, but the admonisher will be disgraced (*Yevamos* 65b). (The religious duty to be silent may not fulfill the mitzvah of offering criticism, but rather the mitzvah that warns against exacerbating divisions among the Jewish people. Still, the duty to be silent is relevant to the "rebuking" mitzvah because it helps the criticizer remember his goal of benefiting the sinner.)

We Often Avoid This

People criticize each other more often than many may realize: Parents criticize their children; spouses criticize each other; coaches criticize their team members; drivers criticize other drivers; and everyone criticizes the government. The details of the mitzvah to "rebuke" can help people criticize with more discretion and sensitivity.

Usually, parents need no urging when it comes to persistence in criticizing their children, but if they keep the "rebuking" mitzvah in mind, they will more easily avoid becoming exasperated at constantly having to repeat themselves. They could view the need for constant repetition as a special opportunity to regularly perform a mitzvah to its extreme. Aside from the inner calm that such a perspective might engender, consciousness of a mitzvah being performed to the extreme will surely result in an appropriate, and equally extreme, reward of miles to Heaven!

Keeping the mitzvah in mind can also lead to more effective parenting. It is not unusual for parents to resort to nagging. To nag is to repeatedly comment on the same behavior, often in the same way, with little or no result. To avoid this common error, parents should remain mindful of the Rabbis' teaching to be silent when it is clear that words will not be heeded. To be silent is a requirement, not an option, because when the child is not benefiting, the parent is not benefiting, either, and is in fact disgracing himself by diminishing his own authority.

Spouses, too, rarely hesitate to criticize one another. They may criticize each other more privately and carefully than they would their children if only to preserve domestic civility, but they should also keep the mitzvah in mind to earn the reward miles!

For new marriages or even new friendships, mitzvah consciousness can produce immediate benefits. Sometimes, just the need to criticize can make a person flustered ("Doesn't she realize ...?" "How could he forget ...?"), and potentially endanger the budding relationship. Recognizing the opportunity to accomplish a mitzvah—and, of course, mitzvos often require some effort—might minimize the resentment and allow the admonisher to concentrate instead on fine-tuning his efforts at building the marriage and/or friendship. Examples of such efforts include contemplating the underlying reason for the other person's bad behavior and identifying exactly how to change the behavior.

On the other hand, by keeping in mind the ultimate goal of criticism (changing sinful behavior), a critic might realize that much of his criticism is unnecessary. That is, he might find that he was criticizing behavior because he didn't like it, rather than because it was immoral or harmful. Such a realization might teach him to become more accepting of the innocuous habits of his spouse and close friends, which will save him a great deal of unnecessary strife. He will also expand his personal boundaries of acceptance, an accomplishment that alone would justify mitzvah-consciousness as a means of gaining reward miles to Heaven. After all, won't the experience of Heaven require all people to expand their personal boundaries?

an ADDED BENEFIT

As previously noted, most people are regular critics, sometimes as employers, sometimes as coaches, sometimes as drivers and very often as wannabe politicians, who could certainly (they claim) do things better. These are not examples of the mitzvah to rebuke sinful behavior.

Sometimes a person has a professional or civic responsibility to criticize; sometimes only a right. In all of these cases, the critic faces a danger: He might criticize just to vent his frustrations. If he is venting his frustrations, he might yell, scream and curse, either at the person he is criticizing or at the world at large. He acts this way because he is feeling overpowered and victimized. Complaining, yelling and cursing may temporarily offset his feelings of victimization, but afterwards, he is more victimized than ever for having confirmed his role as victim.

The Torah's instructions regarding the mitzvah of criticism provide an antidote to the danger of self-victimization. When someone criticizes, whether out of professional or civic duty or because he wishes to indulge his right, he should begin in a helpful manner that is sensitive to the dignity of the person he is addressing. Focusing on sensitivity will control when and how he engages the vortex of life that swirls around him, rather than allowing it to control him. Regularly performing the mitzvah to rebuke with conscious awareness will help to develop this talent.

PUT IT INTO ACTION!

Have in mind the mitzvah of "Speak Up and Speak Out, but Speak Softly" when:

- You properly criticize the behavior or attitude of a family member or friend.
- You find it necessary to criticize a subordinate at work for poor performance.

Notes and Observations

לֹא־תִשְׂנָא אֶת־אָחִיךָ בִּלְבָבֶךָ

"You shall not hate your brother in your heart"
(Lev. 19:17)

Do Not Hate Your Brother in Your Heart

The Basic Instruction

Just before encouraging disapproval of bad behavior, the Torah states, "Do not hate your brother in your heart" (Lev. 19:17). From this part of the verse comes a mitzvah that the Chofetz Chaim presents as his 78th negative, and the *Chinuch* discusses under mitzvah number 238. However, the two sources do not seem to agree on a basic description of the mitzvah, nor does either source echo the words of the Rambam (*Hilchos Deos* 6:5), which both sources usually do. Perhaps, instead, their words echo the troubling connotations of the verse.

Hate is an intense emotion with very negative ramifications; one might expect the Torah to forbid it unequivocally. It is troubling, therefore, to detect seeming limitations to the prohibition. Since the verse says, "You shall not hate your brother," are strangers fair game? The verse says, "in your heart," but is any other body part capable of hating? If the phrase "in your heart" means "secretly," as in, "You shall not hate your brother in secret," the verse begs an even more troubling question: Is open, naked hatred acceptable?

These questions highlight the need to understand the verse on several different levels. Indeed, the verse has no single, self-evident translation. For example, two translations of the Hebrew word, "*sinah*," are "dislike" and "hate," each of which conjures up a different scenario; the translation "resentment" conjures yet a third.

Let's Discuss "*Sinah*" as "Dislike" – Don't Dislike For No Real Reason

The translation, "dislike," conveys the mildest form of *sinah*. Dislike suggests animosity based on differences of opinion or style, rather than on differences of substance. A person might instantly dislike another person without even knowing why. He might not like the other person's style of dress, speech or mannerisms; or perhaps the person just seems too assertive, too meek, too different or too quaint. None of that person's behaviors are wrong, per se, just unappealing.

Disliking people for no real reason is absolutely forbidden; it is the opposite of, "Love your neighbor as yourself," and the opposite of the Almighty's attitude toward humanity. When we translate "*sinah*" as "dislike," the verse becomes, "Do not dislike your brother with your heart." The key phrase here is, "with your heart." The Torah uses the word "heart" to refer to desire, like when it proclaims, "Do not stray after your heart" (Num. 15:39). The Torah is not assuming that the heart is the organ of desire, but rather that both the heart and the sum of our desires constitute a center point: The heart is a person's physical center, while the sum of his desires, his likes and dislikes, form his personality center. Accordingly, the verse, "Do not dislike your brother with your heart," instructs that a person should not use the uniqueness of his personality, his particular blend of likes and dislikes, to cut himself off from another human. On the contrary, each person is unique because he is meant to connect and harmonize with the rest of humanity in a unique way.

We Often Avoid This

The Torah has an antidote for an irrational dislike of another person. The antidote is: Don't keep it in your heart; don't be silent. Once a person forces himself to converse with those who make him uncomfortable, he finds his unfounded antagonism receding. People often force themselves to converse when they would rather not; it's common courtesy to engage with those who might seem strange, even if the conversation is unappealing and, perhaps, avoidable. When engaged in such a conversation, it is important to remember the mitzvah, "Do not dislike your brother with your heart." Not only will mitzvah consciousness garner reward miles to Heaven, but it will make the person who is being courteous aware of his courtesy, thereby elevating a mindless gesture to a powerful posture of grace and kindness. He will also benefit immediately from the education he automatically receives upon understanding another's viewpoint even though he may ultimately reject that viewpoint.

WE COULD REBUILD *the* TEMPLE

The Sages teach that "*sinas chinam*" directly caused the destruction of the Temple, and continues to prevent Mashiach from arriving. If "*sinas chinam*" means "baseless hatred," as it is commonly translated, then this teaching is problematic for three reasons. First, who hates for no reason? I can think of many people who harbor hatreds for reasons with which I do not agree, but I have to concede that their reasons exist. So who were these deplorably primitive people who hated so baselessly that they destroyed the Temple? More importantly, who are their modern counterparts who are preventing the golden age of Mashiach? "Certainly not I," everyone says. Second, hating without reason is irrational, by definition, so why would the Sages bother addressing irrational people? They would have known that irrational people cannot be persuaded. Third, both the Temple and Mashiach symbolize the fullest implementation of Jewish teaching and values. Is the eradication of baseless hatred really all that is missing from the achievement of such a sublime ideal? Indeed, why is the Temple's rebuilding connected with the golden era of Mashiach? Is the Temple just a monument to its cause, as other monuments are to theirs?

Translating "*sinas chinam*" as "baseless dislike" makes the first two problems fall away. The people that lived when the Temple was destroyed were no different from people today. Just like people today, Person A of over 2,000 years ago disliked Person B of over 2,000 years ago for no real reason. Both Person A of today and Person A of 70 C.E. have *sinas chinam*, baseless dislike. The Sages imparted a timeless insight.

The only question left to answer is why baseless dislike would have been the primary cause for the Temple's catastrophic destruction. The Temple was the only place where the Almighty continually manifested His presence in this world. *Pirkei Avos* 5:8 describes the ten miracles that were constantly visible at the Temple. Like the Temple, Man is also a manifestation of the Almighty in this world because Man is created in G-d's image (even though He is not usually visible therein).

How is it possible that finite, corporeal Man could reflect the image of infinite G-d? One answer lies in the image of G-d as One: Because G-d is not divided, mankind can reflect Him by eschewing its natural divisions and uniting. Beyond merely reflecting the image of One

G-d, uniting allows people to imitate G-d. Just as G-d harmonized many different forces to create nature, so must mankind unite by harmonizing many different talents and preferences. Uniting mankind is not easy and is certainly G-d-like. It requires an abiding truth of sufficient complexity, with which all can agree and in which all can participate. Only G-d can provide such a truth, and He has, in the form of a moral certainty called the Torah.

When mankind comes together or even attempts to come together, seeking to reconcile all its disparate talents and preferences in pursuit of this moral certainty, it attests to the existence of One G-d. Under such circumstances, mankind needs and deserves a physical manifestation of G-d's truth to encourage mankind's steadfast efforts. The Temple provided such encouragement. When mankind fails to find ways to bond with each other, they no longer qualify for such encouragement. Rather than preserve the Temple as a parody of its true value, G-d allowed for its destruction.

Let's Discuss *"Sinah"* as "Hate" – Don't Hate Quietly

Above, I presented the verse, "Do not dislike your brother," understanding "brother" in the colloquial sense (i.e., the brotherhood of man). The Rabbis' term for this is, "a brother in mitzvos." The implication of that term is that as long as someone is a responsible member of the Jewish community, other Jews may not dislike him.

On the other hand, when a person rejects community membership by willfully violating its standards, he is no longer a brother in mitzvos. In regard to such people, the verse might read, "Do not hate the one who was your brother (just) with your heart; forcefully rebuke him." In this version, the mitzvah is not leading us away from a certain behavior, but toward one. The Torah is saying that when someone's behavior is both sinful and antisocial, other Jews must express their opposition as vigorously as possible. Such expression involves two steps: First, we as committed Jews must criticize the sin. Second, we must hate the sinner. In this context, hate is positive because it is directed against evil. It is not enough to dislike evil or resent it; we must exert more energy than that, and hate it. The Rabbis even explain the obligation to sometimes include publicly denouncing and ostracizing a sinner who persists in his evil ways.

We Do This All the Time!

In modern society, most people's wrong behaviors are not evil, but merely careless or indulgent ("Everybody's doing it," or, "I couldn't help myself"). Generally, people only personally experience evil if they encounter a bully. According to the Torah, if you encounter a bully, you should stand your ground, explain your opposition and solicit public support.

Many sources would offer the same advice, but seeing that advice expressed in the Torah can give us the added courage to heed it. It could abort further development of a future despot.

Although the opportunity to personally fight evil may be rare, the opportunity to do so in third-party mode is common. For example, out of passionate indignity towards some group or individual who clearly opposes the Torah, many people organize or attend rallies to denounce such behavior. Some may be moved to write letters to the editor. These actions conform to the interpretation, "Do not hate the one who was your brother (just) with your heart; forcefully rebuke him." If we keep the mitzvah in mind while attending the rally or writing the letter, we will earn reward miles to Heaven for an activity that we might pursue with passion anyway.

More immediately, we may also benefit from making better use of our time and energy by focusing on performing the mitzvah, rather than getting mired in the details of the activity. Remembering that the value of a rally lies in the number of people showing up, one could actively connect with other rally-goers to plan future actions rather than just passively listen to speeches; or one could ensure that communal prayers are said; or, at the very least, one could say them alone. Similarly, remembering that the value in writing a letter to the editor lies in the readership, one could spend more time in contacting friends to join a write-in campaign rather than spend too long (as I sometimes do) trying to compose the perfect paragraph that may never get printed. Whenever the mitzvah is the focus of the activity, the time spent is sure to become better justified.

One way to oppose evil in third-party mode is to provide financial support to those who actually carry out the work. However, we should not confuse the mitzvah to give such financial support with the mitzvah to give charity; they are not the same. Each separate mitzvah requires conscious intent toward that specific mitzvah. Properly focused consciousness not only maximizes the reward; it maximizes the mitzvah itself. More importantly, if we confuse the two mitzvos, we risk confusing the performance requirements. For example, the organization MADD (Mothers Against Drunk Drivers) opposes evil in the form of drunk drivers who habitually endanger others. However, MADD is not a charity because it does not alleviate poverty. Therefore, contributions to MADD should not come from one's charity budget. On the other hand, we should not withhold a contribution just because our charity budget has already been allocated. Contributing to MADD or, to give an even more urgent example, contributing to funds for fighting terrorism, requires a decision process that is different from the decision process we might use when contributing to charity.

Knowing that evil exists is often depressing. Understanding the duties we have when faced with evil provides the clarity and confidence to persevere—an immediate reward mile!

Let's Discuss *"Sinah"* as "Resentment" – Don't Stifle Resentment

Interpersonal conflicts often arise when one person offends the other's standards, perhaps by acting in a disappointing way. For example, a person who is punctual might resent someone who arrives fifteen minutes late. The offended party might overlook the offense and put it out of his mind. According to Torah, such graciousness is preferable. Still, some behaviors are inarguably impolite, insensitive or downright offensive. In response to those behaviors, the offended party might respond by saying, "I hate it when …" Probably, he isn't expressing genuine hatred, but rather something milder, like resentment.

As previously noted, the mitzvah of not bearing a grudge prohibits us from harboring ill feeling over harm that fellow Jews cause us. That mitzvah is about "harboring" ill feeling, which is different from the immediate reaction we have when someone offends us. In the heat of the moment, we often have no time to control ourselves; we just react. The Torah does not hold us responsible for these knee-jerk reactions. (We might be responsible for past negligence in not better preparing for this moment, but the moment itself is beyond our control.) However, the Torah does prohibit us from hiding our resentments: "Do not resent your brother in your heart" (i.e., silently, secretly). The Torah instructs us to communicate our disapproval to someone who has offended us.

Through the "resentment" interpretation of "*sinah*," the Torah teaches that if we cannot overlook an offense and put it out of our mind, it is better to express our resentment than to bottle it up. The Rambam says (*Deos*, 6:5) that the Torah only warns against hating in our hearts; however, a person who beats a colleague or insults him, even though that is improper, does not violate this particular mitzvah. The Torah seems to be nudging us towards a heated argument with the potential for a resolution rather than a long simmering feud.

We Do This All the Time!

People frequently (albeit unconsciously) honor the prohibition against bottling up resentment when they lose their temper with those closest to them. My mother always claimed that the best part of her marital spats was making up afterward. That claim has more depth to it than meets the eye: By definition, intimate relationships require the people involved to have intimate knowledge of each other; such knowledge can only come from honest communication. The most honest communication occurs when your guard is down. Perhaps, then, the Almighty intentionally creates moments that catch us off-guard; perhaps He is offering us the chance to grow together through the honest communication that ensues. Our challenge is to use these opportunities for honest communication to work toward deeper relationships.

The prohibition against bottling up resentment is applicable to interactions with strangers, as well. Even though people don't develop deep relationships with every stranger with whom they take issue, they can nevertheless develop better working relationships through honest communication. The same applies even in the absence of a working relationship. For example, imagine someone sitting in his car, waiting for the signal to change. A young man pulls up alongside, his radio blasting something with so much bass that the person in the first car can feel the vibrations in his seat. The person in the first car can pretend to ignore the music and suffer in silence (the light is changing momentarily anyway), or he can raise the volume on his Torah tape or weather report to give the other driver a taste of his own medicine. (The attention the second driver gets from the latter response would probably delight him.) Lastly, the first person could honk his horn and give the inconsiderate driver an exasperated look while maintaining some semblance of a smile and cupping his hand to his ear, letting the inconsiderate driver know that the volume is unbearable. The inconsiderate driver may not respond, or he may respond immediately, or he may respond in the future by remembering the rebuke and keeping his volume down to avoid offending others. Regardless of the response, at least the offended party has expressed his resentment. The most important thing for the first driver to do is to keep the mitzvah in mind, and recognize that the Almighty has designed every unexpected and unwelcome encounter for His people's growth.

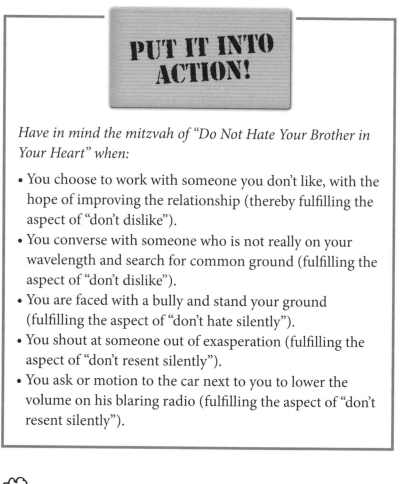

PUT IT INTO ACTION!

Have in mind the mitzvah of "Do Not Hate Your Brother in Your Heart" when:

- You choose to work with someone you don't like, with the hope of improving the relationship (thereby fulfilling the aspect of "don't dislike").
- You converse with someone who is not really on your wavelength and search for common ground (fulfilling the aspect of "don't dislike").
- You are faced with a bully and stand your ground (fulfilling the aspect of "don't hate silently").
- You shout at someone out of exasperation (fulfilling the aspect of "don't resent silently").
- You ask or motion to the car next to you to lower the volume on his blaring radio (fulfilling the aspect of "don't resent silently").

Notes and Observations

וְלֹא־תִשָּׂא עָלָיו חֵטְא

"And do not bear sin because of him" (Lev. 19:17)

Do Not Embarrass People

The Basic Instruction

At the end of the verse that instructs people not to stifle resentment, but to disapprove of bad behavior, the Torah concludes, "and do not bear sin because of him" (Lev. 19:17). The Sages explain this phrase as follows: One must persist with his disapproval of bad behavior, but he may not become sinful about it. That is, he may not go so far as to shame and embarrass the person he is criticizing. The Sages further explain that this mitzvah not to embarrass people applies in all instances, even when people are not criticizing others. The Chofetz Chaim presents this as his 79th negative, and the *Chinuch* discusses it under mitzvah number 240.

Let's Discuss

The Sages identified two progressive stages of shame: In the first stage, the face turns red as blood rushes to the surface. In the second stage, the embarrassment is so acute that the blood drains away from the face, making the face appear white; people call this "looking faint." Because embarrassment, either way, triggers a displacement of blood (a shedding of blood, as it were), the Sages considered inflicting embarrassment on another person a form of murder. The Rambam declared that one who habitually embarrasses others in public so severely that they turn faint loses his share in the World to Come (*Hilchos Teshuvah* 3:14).

Another way to look at shame as a capital crime is to recognize that it "murders" a person's self-esteem. Perhaps for this reason, the *Chinuch* labels shame the worst possible form of human anguish. The *Chinuch* also suggests that, no matter the justification, if someone reproaches another person's actions or thoughts, that person will suffer some level of embarrassment. Thus, even when it is necessary to reproach, the Torah insists that we do so in a way that will minimize the other person's embarrassment.

Consistent with the notion of embarrassment as a form of murder, the Chofetz Chaim cautions against disgracing people, whether they are of low or high stature. Just as we zealously protect every human life, regardless of station, so must we protect every human ego. Even something as seemingly innocent as calling a person by a nickname is injudicious, if that nickname rankles. The *Chinuch* quotes *Maseches Kesubos* 67b, which states that we should be prepared to endanger ourselves before causing another person shame. This passage suggests that human ego might be more valuable than human life itself!

Despite the high value the Sages placed on the human ego, this need for sensitivity applies only if the issue at hand is a private one between two people. With regard to outright sins (as opposed to interpersonal issues), if the sinner does not repent after private reproach, then the critic should rebuke and shame him publicly. A public rebuke will either force the sinner to reconsider or at least demonstrate to all others that such behavior is unacceptable.

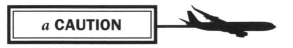

We Often Avoid This

People often avoid embarrassing their loved ones, if only for the selfish reason of preventing confrontations. If they keep the mitzvah, "and do not bear sin because of him," in mind, they can remind themselves how protective the Almighty is, and therefore how protective they should be, of everyone's self-esteem and dignity. Such reminders will lead to reward miles to Heaven.

As communities continue to become more multicultural, people have also become much more careful to avoid embarrassing strangers. Behavior that one culture deems problematic might be acceptable to another culture living in the same neighborhood. Consequently, many are learning to avoid voicing disapproval of certain behaviors that occur in the other culture for fear of appearing culturally insensitive.

a CAUTION

Some of us might even take cultural sensitivity too far, but mitzvah consciousness can help us to refocus. If we fail to address problem behavior for fear of a backlash, we would do well to remember that the Torah advocates criticizing in the same verse that it warns against causing embarrassment; in other words, the two can be compatible. Fortified by that mandate, we should find the resolve and patience to build an effective line of cross-cultural communication. Such resolve and patience will lead to reward miles to Heaven. For example, some communities have expressed resentment for the lewd photographs adorning the covers of magazines for sale at the checkout counters of their local supermarkets.

However, they have expressed their resentment in such a discrete and positive manner that they successfully persuaded some managers to cover up these displays. In this way, they have implemented the two mitzvos of communicating disapproval while not embarrassing, and a third mitzvah, as well: Kiddush Hashem, sanctification of G-d's Name. Even so, such action sometimes leads to criticism from more liberal members of the Jewish community. Such dissension within the Jewish community, though unfortunate, is yet another opportunity to earn reward miles to Heaven: We should stay resolute and patient while fulfilling these mitzvos.

PUT IT INTO ACTION!

Have in mind the mitzvah of "Do Not Embarrass People" when:

- Things are hectic, and you choose to ignore slight offenses.
- You choose *not* to correct the behavior of a family member or friend.
- You refrain from showing up someone who is bragging or stretching the truth.

Notes and Observations

MAINTAIN YOUR ORBIT

The "Golden Rules" teach us how to behave during social interactions, whether or not we chose to have the interactions in the first place. The Torah also provides us with instructions for choosing with whom we interact. We all make choices about our circles of friends and associates. Such choices keenly affect our position in these circles and, consequently, afford many opportunities to collect reward miles to Heaven.

וּבוֹ תִדְבָּק

"And to Him shall you cling"
(Deut. 10:20)

Holy Alliances

The Basic Instruction

The Torah states, "and to Him shall you cling" (Deut. 10:20). The nuance of the Hebrew word for "cling," which is closely related to the word for "glue," implies that we should physically cling to the Almighty. Obviously, physical clinging is impossible because the Almighty is not physical. According to the Sages, we can fulfill this instruction by staying close to those closest with the Almighty, namely, Torah scholars. Those who study and practice the precepts of the Torah gain intimate knowledge of G-d's will; therefore, Torah scholars are closer to G-d than anyone else is.

The mitzvah is thus instructing us to associate with Torah scholars, to form as close a relationship as possible with as many Torah scholars as possible. The Chofetz Chaim discusses this mitzvah under number 16 in his list of positives, and the *Chinuch* discusses it under mitzvah number 434.

Let's Discuss

The Chofetz Chaim explains that people can carry out the mitzvah, "and to Him shall you cling," by marrying into the families of Torah scholars, doing business with Torah scholars, supporting

Torah scholars in their studies and becoming Torah scholars' students and friends. Whoever "clings" in such ways is attached to the Divine Presence. The *Chinuch* explains that those who befriend Torah scholars will ultimately learn the ways of G-d.

This mitzvah teaches us to be on guard against modern society's negative attitude toward clinging. Many people feel that clinging connotes weakness and neediness, which are the opposites of freedom and independence, the avowed cornerstones of modern society. The verse, "and to Him shall you cling," implies that these cornerstones are inconsistent with the Torah perspective and, therefore, not likely valid. People do cling to others, for support, for leadership and for belonging. They just don't necessarily like to acknowledge it. The Torah wants us to acknowledge our common, pervasive human need to "cling," and exercise it with Torah scholars who will help us grow in intelligence and moral fiber.

We Do This All the Time!

We support Torah scholars when we make donations to yeshivas. Such donations should not be viewed simply as charity (a fulfillment of a different mitzvah), for then we might fail to realize that we are also performing the mitzvah, "and to Him shall you cling." By bringing the mitzvah, "and to Him shall you cling," into focus, we will earn extra reward. More immediately, we may become curious about the beneficiaries of our support and therefore become more familiar with them, thereby enhancing our performance of the mitzvah. By the same token, when we pay our synagogue membership, we may be supporting learned, pious rabbis. When we make a donation or pay our dues, we should keep this mitzvah in mind.

We also associate with Torah scholars by attending their study sessions or classes. During our studies, we should keep this mitzvah in mind to earn reward miles for both the mitzvah to cling and the mitzvah to learn.

We Can Do Even Better

Men might consider spending extra time with Torah scholars in their community, and women with the Torah scholars' wives, by socializing with them, offering to do car pools or community projects with them and shopping where they shop.

Often, the wives of Torah scholars run home-based businesses to help support their families. The hidden benefit to patronizing such businesses, even though the prices or selections may not match up to other stores', is the opportunity to visit a scholar's home and to experience the special ambiance, while supporting a Torah scholar.

The suggestion to "marry into the family" of a Torah scholar may seem extreme. Some consider arranged marriages archaic; those people should meet the growing group of parents who do work with their children to find their children spouses. Unfortunately, some also consider it extreme to choose a bride based on the bride's father's Torah scholarship.

Those who consider the idea of arranged marriages archaic should note that most people confine themselves to *some* pool of potential marriage candidates (one's social circle, his friends' social circles, people on his campus, etc.), because they need some method to whittle down the world population to a list of potentially compatible partners. That whittling-down process is much more successful if it is based on carefully selected criteria, rather than on happenstance, availability or chemistry. Furthermore, we should recognize that the Sages, who advised us to "marry into" Torah scholarship, were experts at personal growth and achieving serenity, and following their advice will only be beneficial to us.

In fact, when a person chooses to seek a spouse with a Torah scholar in his or her family, that person is making a statement about how paramount wisdom, spiritual growth and self-discipline are. Recognition of those goals brings the immediate benefit of pursuing the proper course. Should a person succeed in marrying into the family of a Torah scholar, the life-long association will have immense positive influence upon that person. If he is faced with a difficult decision, he will have access to a clear thinker; further, he will have a model of behavior after which he can pattern his own lifestyle choices.

PUT IT INTO ACTION!

Have in mind the mitzvah of "Holy Alliances" when:

- You shmooze with a learned member of the community.
- You patronize a business run by a Torah sage or his wife.
- You seek the advice of a Torah sage, or eavesdrop on his Torah conversation.
- You give charity to support a needy Torah scholar.

Notes and Observations

DAY 10

וְלֹא תִתְחַתֵּן בָּם

"Neither shall you make marriages with them"
(Deut. 7:3)

Do Not Marry Out

The Basic Instruction

With the verse, "neither shall you make marriages with them" (Deut. 7:3), the Torah admonishes against marrying non-Jews. Although the verse specifically refers to the seven nations that originally occupied the land of Israel, according to the Sages, the prohibition extends to all non-Jews. This prohibition is related to the previous mitzvah regarding Torah scholars because non-Jews are the exact opposite of Torah scholars, whom Jews should seek to marry. The Chofetz Chaim lists this mitzvah as the 19th prohibition, and the *Chinuch* discusses it under mitzvah number 427.

Let's Discuss

The *Chinuch* states the obvious: People are deeply influenced by their spouses. A husband or wife without a commitment to Torah values will severely undermine the moral focus of his or her spouse and their children. The words of the *Chinuch* further suggest that the ensuing moral decay of the children will lead to the parents' inconsolable heartbreak.

(The mitzvah only forbids a spouse who does not enter into

the covenant of Israel. A convert is as valid a mate as any other Jew. Indeed, several mitzvos go beyond protecting converts against discrimination by granting them *extra* civil rights.)

The Sages were extremely concerned with the dire ramifications of interfaith marriage. Accordingly, they instituted several rules designed to restrict socializing with non-Jews, thereby minimizing contact that might lead to romantic entanglements. It is beyond the scope of this work to describe the details of these rules. Suffice it to say that, for the most part, the rules relate to food and drink. People eat and drink with those with whom they are closest, and become closest with those with whom they eat and drink. By making restrictions on food and drink, the Sages effectively limited contact between Jews and non-Jews.

Today, people most commonly embrace the spirit of the mitzvah, "neither shall you make marriages with them," when they are abiding by the Rabbinic rules that were instituted to safeguard the mitzvah.

We Often Avoid This

Many of us have close associations with non-Jews, either through work or community. It is not unusual to be invited to participate with non-Jews in food or drink. These invitations can be uncomfortable, partly because of concern for *kashrus* and partly because of a feeling of not really belonging. For these reasons, we might avoid attending a non-Jewish function, or attend, then leave as quickly as possible. It is proper to avoid these occasions or attend them only briefly, because it is imperative to safeguard the mitzvah, in compliance with the authority of the Sages. This realization should help dissipate our discomfort about avoiding or leaving the party, and bolster our behavior with a quiet confidence.

We Often *Help Others* Avoid This

The prohibition against intermarriage seems to leave little opportunity for collecting reward miles. That is, observant Jews have no desire to marry non-Jews, and without desire, the mitzvah is not relevant. A non-observant Jew who would marry a non-Jew, but incidentally marries a Jew instead, has done so for personal reasons, rather than because of the prohibition.

Still, observant Jews who admonish their non-observant relatives, telling them to only date and marry fellow Jews, are behaving in accordance with the mitzvah and should qualify for reward miles. Similarly, those who run programs for Jewish singles, whether they do so professionally or not, are helping others to avoid marrying non-Jews, so they, too, should keep the mitzvah in mind; they surely qualify for reward miles to Heaven. They should also emphasize to their non-observant participants the reward aspect of keeping a mitzvah. Many non-observant Jewish singles refrain from pursuing romance with non-Jews for a variety of reasons, none of which will necessarily last forever. Observant Jews can encourage non-observant Jews' resolve to marry within the faith by applauding their performance of a mitzvah and informing them of the future reward.

Trying to bring two people together can be a maddening experience under any circumstances, but especially when relatives or matchmakers are trying to ensure that non-religious Jews (who do not necessarily disagree with interfaith marriage) marry within the faith. Some insights from the Torah might fortify the efforts of these relatives and matchmakers and help them explain the value of their goals to their subjects.

Genesis 2:24 says, "Therefore a man should leave his father and mother and cleave to his wife." The verse appears to be a Divine dictate, but its meaning may not be clear. Does it mean that the young couple should set up their own household? This has never been the understanding, and many young married couples in many societies live together in their parents' houses without censure. Does it mean that a man should no longer honor or respect his parents if his wife is opposed? On the contrary, Jewish law requires a man to honor and respect his parents, even after their deaths; it is the wife who, if necessary, must relinquish some of her bond with her parents in favor of the honor and respect due her husband. Does it mean, simply, that a man should eventually leave home and get married? The Torah hardly needs to spell that out.

Instead of an instruction, the statement that a man should leave his parents and cleave to his wife seems to be a Divine insight into the nature of Man. It is in the nature of Man to seek a mate from an environment that is different from his own. G-d made Man's nature this way for the same reason that He gave Man life in the first place—not for the purpose of enjoying earthly sensations but for the opportunity of growing worthy of eternal delight. To grow worthy of anything, one must overcome challenges. Getting along with someone different is certainly a challenge, especially on a constant basis (e.g., in a marriage). The Torah describes the role of a wife as "a helpmate, opposite him" (Gen. 2:18), so while seeking pleasure from every interchange with a spouse is a matter of course, one should also anticipate many challenges. Such challenges are unavoidable because the Almighty planned for them; He created people to seek out each other's differences. It is part of human nature.

As people follow their natural tendencies, they soon learn the need for self-discipline. They need food, but too much leads to obesity; they need sleep, but too much leads to lethargy; they need quiet, but too much leads to loneliness; they need excitement, but too much leads to silliness. In this vein, too many differences between spouses can also be harmful; they can lead to too many conflicts or too many compromises. In the pursuit of pleasure, two parties can determine the level of conflict that suits them. However, in the pursuit of growth, they may not always be able to assess which compromises are counter-productive.

As the manual on life, the Torah provides instructions to guide us through difficult issues. The mitzvah not to marry a non-Jew teaches that the compromises of identity and practice one must make to sustain an interfaith marriage work against personal growth. This teaching is the opposite of conventional wisdom, which is precisely why we need the Torah. Conventional wisdom would suggest that one could grow remarkably by adapting to someone from another faith. The Torah disagrees: Rather than grow, one would simply change, and the change would be for the worse. A Jewish spouse promotes positive personal growth; a non-Jewish spouse promotes change of the Jew's inner core, which is a bad thing.

This mitzvah, its reward miles and its lessons can better prepare relatives and professionals for overcoming any despair they may experience from setbacks in their matchmaking efforts.

PUT IT INTO ACTION!

Have in mind the mitzvah of "Do Not Marry Out" when:

- You avoid or minimize social time with non-Jewish co-workers (e.g., at an office party).
- You encourage non-religious relatives to convey their expectations of marrying Jewish to their children.
- You volunteer the name of one Jewish single to another.

Notes and Observations

וַאֲהַבְתֶּם אֶת הַגֵּר

"You should love the stranger"
(Deut. 10:19)

Love the Stranger

The Basic Instruction

When describing the Almighty, Moshe declares that He ensures justice for the orphan and the widow, and He loves the stranger by providing him with food and clothing (Deut. 10:18). The next verse continues, "Therefore, you should love the stranger, for you have been strangers in the land of Egypt." From this verse comes the instruction to love a convert to Judaism. The Chofetz Chaim presents this as the 61st in his list of positives, and the *Chinuch* discusses it under mitzvah number 431.

Let's Discuss

The *Chinuch* points out that there is already an obligation to love a convert from the mitzvah, "Love your neighbor as yourself." (That mitzvah applies to him because a convert has become a fellow Jew.) The Torah adds the mitzvah, "Therefore, you should love the stranger, for you have been strangers in the land of Egypt," to emphasize the duty toward converts. The *Chinuch* goes on to say that this emphasis teaches us to be especially hospitable toward any stranger, such as a Jew (not necessarily a convert) from another town.

The *Chinuch* does not claim that such hospitality is implicit in the mitzvah, only that it is an appropriate derivation. The Chofetz Chaim, however, declares that the Hebrew word "*ger*" (the word in the verse above that means "convert") literally means "stranger," and that the verse mentions a convert simply because a convert is the most extreme example of a stranger. Thus, the Chofetz Chaim's interpretation of the mitzvah requires us to be especially sensitive to any stranger to the community.

We Do This All the Time!

The opportunity to perform the "love the stranger" mitzvah is common, and people often take advantage of it by welcoming the new neighbor; the new member of the synagogue, club or class; or the new relative who has just married into the family. All of these people probably feel a little lost in their new surroundings, and just a greeting and a warm smile takes the edge off their apprehension. When we ease the "stranger's" apprehension, we have performed this mitzvah. We should keep the mitzvah in mind! Every additional effort we extend to help the newcomer acclimate (showing him around, inviting him over or introducing him to others) is a superlative performance. We should remember that the mitzvah is our primary reason for "loving the stranger."

Even though the examples cited above are probably the most common means of participating in the mitzvah to love strangers, today opportunities to fulfill the mitzvah in the classic sense occur with increasing frequency since many people are converting to Judaism out of sincere conviction. The mitzvah teaches us to warmly embrace those who exchange everything with which they are familiar for the chance to enter into the covenant of the Jewish people with the Divine.

Another opportunity to fulfill this mitzvah is with native Jews who have "returned to the fold" (*Baalei Teshuvah*, in the Jewish vernacular). They, too, have left behind their upbringings, their lifestyles, most likely their friends and sometimes even a few family relationships, so they qualify as much as newly converted Jews for a warm embrace and extra attention. It is important for those of us who have always been observant to make them feel completely welcome and at home within their new surroundings. Many of us already actively welcome *Baalei Teshuvah* because they are new additions to our community and synagogue. However, we can intensify our efforts and earn even more reward miles by recognizing *Baalei Teshuvah* as both strangers and "converts."

PUT IT INTO ACTION!

Have in mind the mitzvah of "Love the Stranger" when:

- At a simcha, you are welcoming and friendly to out-of-town guests.
- You greet someone new in shul, make them feel welcome, find them a seat or give them an aliya.
- You show new employees where to get coffee or how to fill out a time sheet.
- You encourage a shy member of a group to join in a group picture.

Notes and Observations

מִפְּנֵי שֵׂיבָה תָּקוּם וְהָדַרְתָּ פְּנֵי זָקֵן

"You shall rise up before a man of hoary head and honor the presence of an old man" (Lev. 19:32)

Raise Them High

The Basic Instruction

The Torah states, "You shall rise up before a man of hoary head and honor the presence of an old man" (Lev. 19:32). This verse is an instruction to honor wisdom by honoring wise people. The Chofetz Chaim presents this mitzvah as number 17 in his list of positives, and the *Chinuch* discusses it under mitzvah number 257.

Let's Discuss

The Torah teaches that anyone who is seventy years old or more, from any background, has learned something about the Creator through life's experiences. We can honor that wisdom by honoring that elder, so the Torah instructs us to rise from our seat. Similarly, a Torah scholar, even one younger than seventy, has learned a great deal about the Creator through the study of Torah. Again, we honor that wisdom by honoring that scholar and, in this case, the Torah instructs us not just to rise, but to rise to full height. (However, if either the elderly person or the scholar behaves immorally, no one should honor him.) The *Chinuch* explains that when we recognize the honor due to a person with wisdom about the Creator, we will be inspired to achieve that wisdom ourselves. (It seems like the *Chinuch* was describing an immediate reward mile!)

Honor and respect are two different things, and obedience is yet a third thing. The mitzvah to honor does not instruct us to *obey* elders, or even Torah scholars. (A different mitzvah addresses obeying a valid Jewish court, which would be composed of Torah scholars.) Neither does the mitzvah instruct us to *respect* elders and Torah scholars. The mitzvah focuses solely on honor. The mitzvos regarding parents address the difference between honor and respect. The mitzvah to honor one's parents requires us to rise for our parents, accompany them and ensure that their needs are satisfied. The mitzvah to respect (also translated as "revere" or "fear") parents warns against occupying our parents' regular spot (e.g., head of the table or favorite easy chair), contradicting our parents and calling them by their names. Possibly, the difference between honor and respect is as follows: One honors a person by giving him something he doesn't have, e.g., food, drink and accompaniment; one respects a person by not taking away what he already has, e.g., his position, authority or seniority. Rising before someone gives him a dignity that he wouldn't otherwise have. Acquiring such dignity is an honor.

We Do This All the Time!

Many people rise for an elderly person or a scholar. People often perform these gestures out of courtesy, or because other people in the room are doing them. Unquestionably, people learned these gestures from their parents, and their parents' inspiration came from the mitzvah. While good habits (i.e., standing to honor someone) are worthwhile, conscious compliance is even better: If we are conscious of this mitzvah, we will have greater energy to rise and more dignity as we do so; and ultimately, we will receive a greater reward.

We Can Do Even Better

Standing is not the only way to honor someone. We can perform this mitzvah in other ways. For example, if we have many telephone messages to return and one of those messages is from an elder, we could return that call first. If we are in a service business, we could serve an elder first or with extra courtesy. Often, a Torah scholar will spearhead a solicitation for charity funds; when solicited by that scholar, whether or not we are able to make a donation, we could respond to the request with a polite note. These are just some examples of ways to more frequently honor those with wisdom about the Creator. As the *Chinuch* has taught, the more often we give such honor, the more motivated we will become to acquire such wisdom—an immediate reward mile!

PUT IT INTO ACTION!

Have in mind the mitzvah of "Raise Them High" when:

- You give a ride to a senior.
- You show deference to senior employees and co-workers.
- You assist a senior in any way.

Notes and Observations

וּמִקְדָּשִׁי תִּירָאוּ

"My sanctuary you shall revere; I am G-d"
(Lev. 19:30)

Respect the Sanctuary; Don't Enter While *Tamei*

The Basic Instruction

The Torah statement, "My sanctuary you shall revere, I am G-d" (Lev. 19:30), instructs us to stand in awe and reverence of the Temple, and, now that the Temple has been destroyed, of its site. The Chofetz Chaim comments on this instruction under number 18 in his list of positive mitzvos, while the *Chinuch* discusses it under mitzvah number 254.

The Torah gives a related prohibition with the statement, "If there is anyone among you who is not '*tahor*' (clean) ... he shall not come within the camp" (Deut. 23:11). Based on the teachings of the Sages, we infer that the "camp," today, is the site of the Temple. The instruction forbids anyone who is "*tamei mais*" (ritually impure due to contact with a corpse) to enter the Temple site. The Chofetz Chaim lists this as the 193rd in his list of prohibitions, and the *Chinuch* discusses it under mitzvah number 565.

A number of other mitzvos are closely related to these, but because the Chofetz Chaim does not consider them applicable today, I have not presented them here in detail. However, the following list will guide the reader who wishes to better research the awe and reverence due the Temple and its site. The *Chinuch* discusses related mitzvos under numbers 184 ("Kohanim should enter the inner sanctuary only for service purposes"), 362 ("Send the ritually unclean outside the camp of the Divine Presence"), and 363 ("Do not enter any part of the sanctuary while ritually unclean").

Let's Discuss

The *Chinuch* records the Talmud's description of irreverence: It is irreverent to enter the Temple Mount with a walking stick, with shoes or the dust of travel on one's feet, or with a money bag. Furthermore, one should not spit on the Temple Mount, pass through the Temple as a shortcut, or enter the Temple Mount for any reason other than the purpose of performing a mitzvah (after which one should retreat by walking backwards little by little). Even when not on the Temple mount , one should neither sleep nor relieve himself while facing east or west because the Temple sat on that axis. (This rule pertains to an open field in which the person appears to be pointing towards the Temple; it does not apply if the person appears to be facing a partition). A person should also avoid building a home, porch or courtyard modeled after the corresponding part of the Temple.

The above describes the rules for adhering to the positive instruction, "My sanctuary you shall revere." Since the described behaviors are all prohibitive, whereas the mitzvah itself is active, we must conclude that one is fulfilling the mitzvah when he is actively preventing violation of it. For example, if one purposefully removes his shoes before entering the Temple site, he is fulfilling the mitzvah.

Today, the only opportunity we have to fulfill the mitzvah of awe and reverence is to refrain from entering the Temple site. The prohibition forbids us from entering the site while in the state of "*tamei mais*" (ritual impurity) that we are in today. (We have reached this state because most of us have been in hospitals, and have therefore been too close to corpses.) Anyone who wants to enter the Temple site (and unfortunately, many tour groups do), but refrains because of the Torah instruction, is honoring the prohibitive mitzvah.

Although the prohibition from entering the Temple site keeps us from demonstrating our reverence for the site directly, the Chofetz Chaim maintains that we can and need to demonstrate our reverence indirectly. He cites the verse, "... yet have I been to them as a little sanctuary" (Ezekiel 11:16), to show that we should behave with reverence inside synagogues and Torah study halls ("little sanctuaries"). Behaving with reverence means refraining from frivolity, idle talk, business calculations and sleeping.

We Do This All the Time!

Most people approach the Western Wall with a great deal of reverence because of its antiquity and because of what it represents. Maintaining awareness of our reverence will infuse our performance of the mitzvah with greater significance. For Jews who live in Israel and can visit the Wall frequently, such awareness will help them maintain the proper attitude and avoid desensitization.

Although, strictly speaking, the mitzvah does not apply to the plaza in front of the Western Wall (which is not technically part of the Temple site), the Chofetz Chaim explains that the mitzvah applies to every synagogue and Torah study hall. Therefore, the mitzvah certainly covers the Western Wall plaza, one of the largest and most famous synagogues and Torah study halls in the world.

Whether at the Western Wall plaza or in our own community synagogues and Torah study halls, we are performing a mitzvah each time we aim to behave in accordance with the sanctity of the place. When we resist the temptation to act inappropriately (i.e., talking business, telling jokes or cutting through the "sanctuary" en route to another destination), we are fulfilling the mitzvah to an even greater degree. Refraining from discussing sports is an especially profound performance of the mitzvah: Such self-control sets an example for the many people who forget that discussing sports is inappropriate. Sometimes, we avoid discussing sports inside the synagogue just because we are concerned about appearing irreverent to our friends or our Rabbi. Reminding ourselves that exercising such restraint is also the fulfillment of a mitzvah will both elevate our self-esteem by allowing us to relish our own self-discipline and give us the sublime feeling of showing respect to the Almighty. These rewards are but small portions of the immense reward to which consistent mitzvah-consciousness will lead.

One should never underestimate the benefit of demonstrating respect to the Almighty through His places of worship and study. Rav Noach Weinberg of Aish HaTorah tells a true story of how one such show of respect led to a complete transformation: One day, a highly intelligent, Harvard-educated but completely assimilated tourist in Jerusalem found himself walking backwards from the Western Wall to the plaza. He later explained that he had been so struck by the Wall that he had uttered a prayer to G-d, even though he didn't believe in Him. "G-d," he said to himself, "I don't know anything about You or even if You are there, but I am here and I feel something, so if You are there, please introduce Yourself to me."

It was a serious prayer because he had been courting a non-Jewish girl and could sense that becoming seriously involved with her would lead him to completely abdicate any last vestige of his Jewishness. When he finished his prayer, he started walking backwards because he had noticed others doing so and wanted to show the same respect. ("When in Rome," he figured.) It was while he was respectfully walking backwards that Rabbi Schuster of Heritage House, who regularly scans the crowd at the Western Wall, looking for people who might be interested in learning more about their Judaism, caught sight of him. He tapped the young man on the shoulder and asked him if he was interested in seeing a yeshiva. Startled by the intrusion into his thoughts, the young man exclaimed, "What the blankety-blank is a yeshiva?" Equally startled by the tourist's intense reaction because he was not aware of the prayerful reverie he was interrupting, the rabbi stammered back, "It's a place where you learn about G-d."

The young man was stunned. He had just uttered the first real prayer of his life, asking for an introduction to G-d, and here was an invitation to visit a yeshiva and learn about G-d. He felt compelled to accept. At the yeshiva, he met Rav Noach Weinberg, who was so enlightening that the young tourist changed his plans and enrolled in a summer course the rabbi was teaching. This led to other changes in the man's life, which in turn led to more changes, until he had significantly strengthened his commitment to Judaism. Over time, as a result of this series of events, he eventually met a Jewish girl who turned out to be his true love, and with whom he is now living happily ever after.

The young man's entire transformation stemmed from a sincere prayer and a single demonstration of heartfelt respect for the Almighty's Temple. Clearly, the power of a mitzvah performed with genuine intent is beyond measure.

PUT IT INTO ACTION!

Have in mind the mitzvah of "Respect the Sanctuary" when:

- You approach the Western Wall.
- In a shul or beis midrash, you behave in accordance with the sanctity of the place and resist the temptation to act inappropriately.

Notes and Observations

וְלֹא תְחָנֵּם

"Nor shall you show them mercy"
(Deut. 7:2)

Do Not Favor Evil People

The Basic Instruction

At the other end of the spectrum are people that we are not supposed to honor: evil people. In fact, we should not even take pity on evil people. The Torah delivers this mitzvah with the verse, "nor shall you show them mercy" (Deut. 7:2). The Chofetz Chaim presents this as the 20th in his list of negatives, and the *Chinuch* discusses it under mitzvah number 426.

Let's Discuss

The actual Torah verse refers to an idol worshiper, but the *Chinuch* extends the prohibition against taking pity on anyone who ignores the Almighty's seven Noahide laws, which the *Chinuch* lists as follows:

1. Do not worship idols.
2. Do not curse G-d.
3. Do not murder or force someone into a fatal situation (even when the victim is a fetus).
4. Do not commit sexual immorality. (This law bans relations between a man and his mother; a man and his

father's wife, even after the father's death; a man and his sister with whom he shares the same mother; a man and a married woman; a man and another male; and a person and any animal.)

5. Do not rob. (This prohibition includes stealing, kidnapping and dishonest dealings.)
6. Do not eat flesh cut from a living animal.
7. Set up courts to administer these laws.

Most people seem to keep these laws, or at least subscribe to them. However, some do not. Those who do not are immoral and evil. What does the Torah say about how to treat such people? Both the *Chinuch* and Chofetz Chaim explain that we should not render gifts or favors to immoral people, praise immoral people or praise their causes. In fact, we should not consider anything about immoral people positive, not even attributes completely independent of their immorality. For example, if an evil person's physical appearance is pleasant or dignified, we should not comment on it. The *Chinuch* explains that the Torah wants us to treat evil people as pariahs, unfit for society, to ensure that their immoral activities and attitudes do not influence others in any way.

Remarkably, the Chofetz Chaim takes an even more forceful stand. He says that we are not even to help evil people who are in danger. For example, if an evil person is drowning, we should not rescue him; if one is deathly sick, we should not offer him medicine or perform surgery. Nevertheless, it is forbidden to actively harm an evil person (except when necessary to stop an evil act); we must simply remain passive in the face of his predicament. However, if there is reason to fear the results of passivity (i.e., if the failure to act could result in legal repercussions), then we may act. In such instances, we should seek compensation to avoid having done the immoral person a favor for free. Practically speaking, however, we need to be sure that the person at risk is indeed wicked, because if he is not wicked, we must provide assistance.

We Often Avoid This

Who are actual examples of people whom we should avoid at all costs? The most obvious examples are murderers and thieves. One might assume that everyone would avoid showing murderers and thieves favors or kindness, but this is often not the case. Today, we live in a society that is far removed from Torah values. Therefore, we live in danger of succumbing to conventional wisdom, rather than to Torah wisdom. Consider the cases of known criminals who somehow escape conviction due to technicalities. To provide a glaring example, in one case in which police were searching for a missing girl, a landlord helped the police enter every apartment in his building. In one apartment, the police noticed illegal drugs, so they later returned with a search warrant and found over $130,000 worth of illegal drugs. The court disallowed the evidence that showed that the tenants were trafficking drugs because the police had first discovered the drugs during an illegal entry. Of course, the purpose of the "illegal" entry was to protect the life of a young girl. Any sane, moral person would enter the apartment for that purpose. Further, the evidence undeniably established the apartment tenants as drug traffickers, one of the worst blights with which modern society must contend. Those tenants were set free to continue their damage. Those who argue against illegal searches claim that criminals also have rights to privacy. The Torah says they don't.

A Jewish court is not bloodthirsty; it protects the accused from a wrongful verdict more than other judicial systems do. For example, the court will not administer a Torah punishment unless two valid and independent witnesses testify that they personally saw the accused commit the crime, and until someone warns the accused of the punishment and of the witnesses' willingness to testify. Circumstantial evidence is insufficient in a Jewish court, but once valid evidence is in, the accused is guilty.

Giving rights to the guilty is the same as giving the guilty free gifts. Naturally, we are outraged when we learn of such injustice; rightfully, we sometimes protest to our elected representatives. When we protest, we should be conscious of the mitzvah, "nor shall you show them mercy." Mitzvah consciousness will give us added courage, logic and dignity.

We Can Do Even Better

We should shun violators of the other Noahide laws as much as we shun murderers and thieves. The Torah does not distinguish among those laws; they are all of equal significance. For the non-Jew, sexual mores are more liberal than they are for the Jew, but adultery and homosexuality are still forbidden. The Torah does not require us to ferret out those who feel they cannot help themselves but are embarrassed enough to keep their sinful behavior private. Those who sin publicly, however, are vigorously seeking to change society. According to the Torah, they will destroy society. That is very much a concern for us. Unfortunately, today, adultery and homosexuality are so rampant and so public, it would be difficult to marshal an effective opposition. Nevertheless, if we can muster any opposition, we are performing the mitzvah, "nor shall you show them mercy."

Equally difficult to oppose today are those who curse G-d. Many people proclaim G-d non-existent or impotent; no curse against the Almighty is greater. The mass media has embraced this godlessness, and has in turn fashioned conventional wisdom: conventions by which most people live their lives, conventions predicated on the notion that G-d does not exist. In short, for all practical purposes, the liberal segment of western civilization has become godless.

To many, the battle against the godless forces seems hopeless; the opportunity to win any kind of victory, even a small one, seems rare. Such dismay is false, though. The mishnah in *Pirkei Avos* explains that it is our job not to win the war, but to engage in the battle. The mitzvah, "nor shall you show them mercy," is a reminder of the Jewish people's special obligation to distance themselves from negative influences, and to refuse to give those influences credence.

We can distance ourselves from negativity by switching off the radio, changing the channel or turning the newspaper page upon encountering godless sentiments; by writing letters of protest to newspaper editors or canceling a subscription; and by promoting to friends and acquaintances those mass media outlets that are truer to Jewish values. When we remember that we are distancing ourselves from negativity because of the mitzvah (in addition to our personal disgust), we strengthen our conviction that good values will prevail.

PUT IT INTO ACTION!

Have in mind the mitzvah of "Do Not Favor Evil People" when:

- You skip over news stories about wicked people.
- You organize or attend a rally to oppose an anti-Torah idea or policy.

Notes and Observations

DAY 14

GET A LIFE, GIVE A LIFE

The preceding section, *Maintain Your Orbit*, dealt with selecting our social circle, because the relationships we maintain have a profound influence on the kind of lives we lead. However, we don't merely respond to others, we act independently, as well. The colloquial expression for this is "get a life."

When we do develop our lives—our powers, capacities and resources—we often find we want to use these achievements to help others—to "give a life." The Torah provides vital instructions for how to develop the self and how to help others. In both spheres—getting a life and giving a life—maintaining consciousness of the process will surely lend majesty to the results.

וְהָלַכְתָּ בִּדְרָכָיו

"You shall walk in His ways"
(Deut. 28:9)

Be Like G-d

The Basic Instruction

The Torah verse, "you shall walk in His ways" (Deut. 28:9), is an instruction to emulate the ways of the Almighty, to be like G-d. The Chofetz Chaim presents this as the 6th mitzvah in his list of positives, while the *Chinuch* discusses it under mitzvah number 611.

Let's Discuss

To explain the mitzvah, "you shall walk in His ways," the Chofetz Chaim explains that just as the Almighty is called gracious, so should we be gracious; just as He is called compassionate, so should we be; just as He is called holy, so should we be; and so on. Other adjectives used to describe the Almighty in this context are humble, righteous, straightforward, guileless, resolute, kind and patient. The mitzvah enjoins us to develop all of these character traits. More importantly, the mitzvah reveals the essence of spirituality: One who acquires these traits will be G-d-like!

Since G-d is infinite, it follows that the bounds of this mitzvah, to emulate Him, must also be near infinite. Accordingly, we should not have to completely master these character traits in order to fulfill the mitzvah; that would be impossible. Rather, each step we take toward mastering these character traits is a performance of the mitzvah.

We Do This All the Time!

People "walk in His ways" all the time! People are kind, courteous and honest, and have compassion for those in trouble; but they are raised to act that way, so it's not really an accomplishment. However, if we remain mindful that the Almighty is the original model for these character traits, and that He wants His people to emulate Him, we may acquire for ourselves a wonderful spot in the World to Come. We should be conscious of the mitzvah to "walk in His ways" whenever we help others, act courteously, show compassion or answer honestly. Hundreds of actions every day could become mitzvos if we simply reminded ourselves that we are emulating the Almighty. Such awareness would also help us further develop these positive attitudes, allowing us to claim them as our own accomplishments.

According to the Sages, humility is the most prominent aspect of the Almighty, and wherever we find humility, we will find G-d. This may seem strange; the words "almighty" and "humble" do not normally go together. The key to understanding what the Sages meant lies in the meaning of humility. By "humble," the Sages did not mean bereft of power or ability; they meant willing to forgo ability and desire in favor of someone else. The infinite Almighty was and is willing to forgo His ability and desire in order to allow frail Man his independence. Parents experience this sense of humility when they let go of the toddler they would rather coddle, and let the toddler fall so that he or she can learn to walk. Accordingly, parents "walk in His ways" every time they let go and exercise humility (the first day of school, the first time the parent doesn't hold the back of the child's bicycle, the first time the child goes to overnight camp, the first time the child gets the car keys, the first time he goes to Israel to study, the walk down the aisle to the *chupah*). Upon each of these occasions and many others like them, the awareness that we are performing the mitzvah of being like G-d invokes a feeling that is nothing short of divine. We experience immediate reward miles.

Similarly, we acquire some humility from our own experiences when we accept another's choices as superior to our own, particularly in our careers or in our marriages. We can turn those humbling moments into positive experiences by remembering that the experiences help us emulate the Almighty. We can earn untold reward in the process, and the accomplishment will be completely our own.

Let's Discuss, Again

The *Chinuch* first explains the mitzvah to "walk in His ways" the way the Chofetz Chaim explains it (just as the Almighty is called gracious, so should people be gracious, etc.), but toward the end of his discussion, the *Chinuch* paraphrases the Rambam's *Hilchos Deos*, explaining the mitzvah as an instruction to follow the "golden mean" (the middle of two extremes). That is, each character trait has a continuum with extremes at either end (i.e., lazy to hyperactive, stingy to overly generous). According to this interpretation of the mitzvah, one should not indulge in the extremes, but rather behave according to the golden mean or the middle path: not lazy, but not hyperactive, either; not stingy, but not overly generous, either; and so on.

I have always had two questions about this explanation. First, how does this idea follow from the instruction to walk in His ways? Second and more important, how is one to identify the exact middle path between two extremes? The *Chinuch* provides no definition of "middle," and no definition seems feasible given the infinite number of possible situations. Without a definition or description, each person is bound to draw a different conclusion based on his or her natural inclinations. For example, someone who is naturally stingy might consider a one-dollar handout to a panhandler quite munificent, while someone who is naturally generous might consider a dollar to be the bare minimum.

In *Darash Moshe*, Rav Moshe Feinstein, *zt"l*, suggests a novel and satisfying approach to this dilemma. His comments on the phrase, "*Zos chukas haTorah*" ("This is the decree of the Torah"), in *Parshas Chukas*, seem to encourage not the middle path, but the two opposite extremes, depending on the situation.* For example, with one's own money, a person should be generous, but with someone else's money, he should be stingy; when performing a good deed, one should act energetically, but faced with an unsavory activity, one should be "too lazy" to get involved.

Rav Feinstein's approach suggests that the mitzvah "to walk in His ways" is an instruction to develop the self-discipline necessary to control ourselves, and thus react appropriately to each situation. This makes a lot of sense. If we wish to be like G-d, we must, like G-d, be able to exert control, and the very first thing we should be able to control is ourselves.

We Do This All the Time!

People constantly work on improving their self-control. Examples include diet workshops, exercise regimens, smoking cessation programs, anger management classes and assertiveness training courses. So that they will earn the commensurate reward miles, those enrolled in these programs should realize

* *Darash Moshe* (Mesorah Publications, Ltd., 1994), p. 253

that they are engaged in a mitzvah activity. That realization may also yield a more immediate benefit: greater perseverance in achieving their goals. Many people have more stamina and determination when pursuing goals set by the Torah, rather than ones they set themselves, because their own goals may be unrealistic or less beneficial than they anticipated. When people pursue Torah goals, they can be confident of the goals' worth, and can trust that the Almighty will assist them in attaining them.

Everyone knows that developing self-control is rewarding. By making that development a mitzvah, the Torah implies that the reward is beyond anything anyone can imagine.

Once More, Let's Discuss

The Rambam presents the details of this mitzvah, "Be Like G-d," in the first five chapters of *Hilchos De'os* of the *Mishnah Torah*. Interestingly, within this discussion, in chapter four, the Rambam describes how we must take care of our health. We might justifiably wonder why taking care of our health belongs in a discussion about emulating G-d, who has no body and cannot get sick. The likely answer is that just as G-d is whole in all aspects, so must we strive to be whole—and that starts with maintaining our health. In the Rambam's words, we cannot relate to G-d when we are sick. It follows then, that anything we do to preserve our health is a performance of this mitzvah, especially when we do so for the purpose of fulfilling our Divine mandate. (A very similar theme is expounded in chapter 231 of *Shulchan Aruch, Orech Chaim.*)

We Do This All the Time—Big Time!

We devote an enormous amount of our time, energy and resources to health foods, medications, exercise regimens and diet programs, not to mention the time we spend in waiting rooms to see health professionals. Surely, when we practice these measures guided by the goal of fulfilling our Divine mandate to emulate G-d, we will earn "good health" in the World to Come in addition to whatever health G-d affords us here. Even more immediately, this mitzvah rewards us with a powerful motivation to maintain our personal health and well-being—one more incentive to stick to that exercise routine!

PUT IT INTO ACTION!

Have in mind the mitzvah of "Be Like G-d" when:

- You listen to a troubled friend or family member and express concern and understanding.
- You behave humbly, such as by denying some credit you may deserve, or by soliciting ideas from others even though you are satisfied with your own analysis.
- You control your appetite (fulfilling the self-control aspect).
- You control your anger (fulfilling the self-control aspect).
- You strive to eat a properly balanced meal (fulfilling the staying healthy aspect).
- You take precautions to ensure that you drive safely in a safe vehicle (fulfilling the staying healthy aspect).

Notes and Observations

וְאֹתוֹ תַעֲבֹד

"Him shall you serve"
(Deut. 6:13 and 10:20)

Just Ask G-d

The Basic Instruction

The Torah states, "Him shall you serve" (Deut. 6:13 and 10:20). The Sages point out that the Hebrew word for "serve" in these verses, "*avod*," is the same word used in the verse, "to serve Him with all your heart" (Deut. 11:13), from which we learn that the service required is one of the heart. They further explain that service of the heart refers to prayer. Thus, the Torah is instructing us to pray to G-d. The Chofetz Chaim lists this as the 9th positive mitzvah while the *Chinuch* discusses it under mitzvah number 433.

Let's Discuss

The prayer services that we conduct on a regular basis fulfill this mitzvah, but we should realize that these prayers include more than the mitzvah requires. The mitzvah only requires that we each ask G-d for what we need sometime during each day. However, the *Anshei Knesses HaGedolah*, the most prolific Supreme Court in Jewish history, legislated that we should normally pray three times daily, which clearly suggests that each time we request something from G-d, we are fulfilling the mitzvah. The *Anshei Knesses HaGedolah* also established for us the proper structure of a prayer—the *Amidah*, or *Shemoneh Esrei*. A proper prayer starts by praising the Almighty, continues with one or more requests and finishes with praise and thanks to the Almighty.

We Do This All the Time!

Of course, every time we open the siddur and pray we are fulfilling this mitzvah and we are no doubt aware of it. However, we may not be mindful of the other times we fulfill this mitzvah. Every time we hope something happens or doesn't happen, every time we ask G-d for help, especially when we say it out loud, could really constitute a prayer to the Almighty and thus be a fulfillment of this mitzvah.

"I hope the train comes soon." "I hope I find a parking spot." "I hope the cake turns out right." "I hope the boss likes my presentation." True, these examples might seem too trivial to qualify for prayer, but we should remember that in the grand scheme of things many of our requests probably seem trivial to the Infinite Creator of the Universe. On the other hand, the Infinite Creator has infinite patience and concern for each one of us. Even more than a mother is endlessly interested in her baby, the All Merciful is concerned with us.

When voicing these personal prayers, it's best to follow the guidance of our Sages and express our petitions in the proper format. For example, if we need to get somewhere quickly, instead of mentally hoping the train arrives soon, we could quietly say, "Almighty, You can do anything, so please help me get there on time. And thank you for always looking after me."

It is comforting to be aware that the Almighty has instructed us to request our needs from Him, especially since it suggests that He will fulfill our requests. However, sooner or later, everyone comes to realize that not all requests get filled, even though they may have been very urgent and the intended recipients most deserving. Still, even when our needs are not filled in the manner we wished, we can take comfort on a number of levels. First, by praying, we have performed His will. We have gotten closer to Him and will ultimately receive reward for that. Second, since we have followed G-d's instructions to pray to Him, we might anticipate that He will "look out" for us in a different way if "our way" didn't come to pass. Finally, when we express our hopes and desires as prayer to G-d, we will automatically develop a more positive attitude, that whatever happens thereafter will surely be for the best.

PUT IT INTO ACTION!

Have in mind the mitzvah of "Just Ask G-d" when:

- You concentrate on a particular need during prayers.
- You're looking to find a parking spot, hoping for light traffic conditions or a timely gas station, etc., especially since it will remind you to ask G-d for assistance and help you articulate your prayer properly.

Notes and Observations

וְהִתְוַדּוּ אֶת־חַטָּאתָם

"... they shall then confess their sin ..."
(Num. 5:6-7)

Promise G-d

The Basic Instruction

The Torah states, "When a man or a woman shall commit any of the sins that people do, to commit a breach of faith against G-d, whereupon that soul will be guilty, they shall then confess their sin that they have done" (Num. 5:6). This is the source for the mitzvah to confess one's sin—a declaration known as "Viduy." The Chofetz Chaim lists this as his 33rd positive mitzvah, while the *Chinuch* lists it as mitzvah number 364.

Let's Discuss

The Chofetz Chaim encapsulates this mitzvah with the statement, "A sinner should turn back from his sin and confess his misdeeds before the blessed G-d." This is probably the most common understanding of this mitzvah; it mandates two activities, namely, repentance and confession. However, it is possible that the *Chinuch* disagrees, since he titles the mitzvah, "The precept of confession over sins." Although the *Chinuch* does discuss repentance in his treatment of the mitzvah, in fact stating that it is an absolute prerequisite to the mitzvah, still it is not the mitzvah itself. Perhaps the *Chinuch*'s position is that we do not need a distinct mitzvah to repent, since the "original" one still applies. For example, if someone sinned by eating pork, the *Chinuch* would maintain that no new instruction is needed to tell him to change his ways and not eat pork again, since the original instruction, "Don't eat pork," still applies. When he finally decides to comply with the mitzvah, the only new instruction needed is how to amend his past behavior. The mitzvah being discussed here teaches that in order to amend past behavior a person must confess.

Whether or not repentance itself is included in this mitzvah, it seems that there are two distinct concepts, repentance and Viduy (confession or promise, as shall be explained). Repentance consists of three steps: 1) stopping the sinful activity; 2) regretting ever having done the sin; and 3) committing oneself never to repeat the sin again. If any of these components is missing, the sinner cannot be satisfied that he has repented. For example, if the person resolves never to repeat the act but is not sorry for having eaten the pork (he may be happy that at least now he knows what it tastes like), then he has not repented. The stain of the sin remains. Similarly, if the person truly regrets having eaten pork but realizes that his urge to do so seems uncontrollable and he will probably do it again—as, indeed, he has already done several times in the past—then, again, he has not repented.

This experience of knowing that we will sin again is quite common, if not for eating pork then for a number of other misbehaviors to which we're prone. My rebbi, Rav Yaakov Weinberg, *zt"l*, advised that for such temptations we could still achieve repentance if our resolution focused on combating the ease with which we succumb. That is, we could use our genuine feelings of regret to resolve never to succumb so quickly to the temptation, to instead try to delay for a few hours; or to resolve never to succumb so fully but instead only partially.

I believe that my rebbi's advice was based on a profound insight which I understand with the following analogy: If I want to take a step forward, I must do three things—raise my foot, lean forward and lower my foot. Suppose I raise my foot high and put it down without leaning my body forward. I have done two of the three motions necessary to take a step but I have gone nowhere, because my foot lands in the same place it started. By contrast, if I raise my foot just a little, lean forward just a little and then put it down, I will have taken a small step. Not as large as the step I could have taken, but a step nevertheless. Similarly, repentance requires three components and if any are missing repentance doesn't happen at all. But repentance does occur when each component is present in some measure, however small. In this way, we can satisfy all three components of repentance and proceed to the next step.

The next step consists of three components: 1) we must identify the specific sin, e.g., "I have eaten pork"; 2) we must feel remorse, e.g., "I am sorry I did this" or "I am embarrassed to have ever done such a thing"—the more fully we express our remorse, the better; and 3) we must formulate a new resolve, e.g., " I will never eat pork again," or, in a case of uncontrollable desire as described above, "I will never eat a full ham sandwich again; I will not eat more than half." The first step could certainly be characterized as a confession but the last two components are really promises. For this reason, I have named this mitzvah, "Promise G-d." (Interestingly, the Ramban requires that each component be stated aloud.)

The promises we make must derive from a sense of sincere regret and commitment. Just mouthing the words is useless. At the same time, feelings are not enough to fulfill the mitzvah; we must implement all three components described above. If any part is missing, we have not performed the mitzvah. The reason we recite so many vague, general statements of contrition and resolve on Yom Kippur is because we realize that we are forgetting many of the specifics and must rely on Yom Kippur's special power to effect atonement. However, throughout the year, whenever we regret what we have done and enunciate our resolve to do better, we fulfill this mitzvah of "promising G-d."

We Do This All the Time!

Many times we regret our actions, sometimes immediately and other times upon reflection. For example, whenever we lose our temper and lash out at the people around us, we often regret it soon after. We may even say aloud to ourselves, "Shouldn't have done that!" Another instance might be when we review the day's events with our spouse and admit to some embarrassing behavior that we intend not to repeat. These are fulfillments of the mitzvah and we should keep it in mind! Awareness is especially useful for this mitzvah since it will help us do it properly. Even though the regret is sincere and accompanied by an inner resolve to behave better in the future, we may not naturally do all the necessary steps. Many times, we may not actually say anything at all. But if we remember to articulate the three components of the promise we're supposed to make to G-d (and really to ourselves), we can rest assured that the Divine instruction will help us turn these uncomfortable moments of guilt and shame into powerful vehicles for character development.

PUT IT INTO ACTION!

Have in mind the mitzvah of "Promise G-d" when:

- You do something wrong and regret it, whether immediately or years later. Remember to follow the three essential steps of teshuvah, as well.

Notes and Observations

Transmit Torah

The Basic Instruction

The mitzvah to transmit Torah is ordinarily called, "Learn and Teach Torah." However, for reasons I will detail below, I prefer to call it, "Transmit Torah."

There is no one basic instruction for the mitzvah to transmit Torah. Instead, at least four instructions convey this message:

1) Understand Torah: "You shall study them" (Deut. 5:1).
2) Memorize Torah: "… lest you remove it from your heart"(Deut. 4:9).
3) Schedule daily times for Torah study: "You shall think about it day and night" (Joshua 1:8).
4) Teach Torah: "You shall teach them diligently to your students" (Deut. 6:7).

Each of the four has its own verse and could constitute a separate mitzvah. For example, a person could reach a deep understanding of a particular topic in the Torah, but have to consult notes to remember salient details. Conversely, he could memorize a great deal of Torah information without understanding its import. He could both understand and memorize beautifully without committing to a daily regimen, while, on the other hand, if he studies with a daily regimen, he will not necessarily remember or even understand what he has studied. One could teach, and teach well, without necessarily fulfilling the other three components. (Of course, if one teaches well, he must have at least achieved some understanding of the material that he is teaching, but that understanding may be far weaker than the one he is capable of developing.)

The question that arises is, "Why is there only one mitzvah (to transmit Torah), instead of four?" A famous dictum equates the one mitzvah of transmitting Torah to all 612 of the other mitzvos. Perhaps the Almighty provided only this one mitzvah, encompassing the four components, so that the total would equal all of the other mitzvos, thus underscoring the one mitzvah's importance. If G-d had given four separate mitzvos, none of those would equal all of the others.

The *Chinuch* further develops the answer to the question "Why is there only one mitzvah?" when he describes the mitzvah to transmit Torah, and its goal: The *Chinuch* explains that the goal of the mitzvah is to perceive the ways of G-d (to relate to Him). Our relationship with G-d deepens as our knowledge of Torah deepens. The more Torah we know, the more broadly we can appreciate the Eternal and His Infinity; the more clearly we know the halacha, the more detailed our perception of the Almighty's values. We have a constant need to relate to G-d, but to learn constantly would be impossible! We also need to earn a living, maintain our health, develop our human relationships and prioritize a host of other activities, including rest and relaxation. To acknowledge this, the *Chinuch* emphasizes that we must find at least some time to learn. He thereby identifies learning Torah as a necessity of life, and suggests that we should make it a priority, just as we prioritize food, shelter and rest. Once we realize the importance of the learning component of the mitzvah, we can extend the importance to the other components. If learning were a separate mitzvah, then the necessity to learn may never have served to remind people of the needs to remember and to teach.

A third answer to the question might lie in the title of

the mitzvah: Both the Chofetz Chaim and the *Chinuch* title the mitzvah, "Know Torah and teach it." I have entitled it, "Transmit Torah," because I believe that title evokes the title intended by the Rambam. In *Yad HaChazaka*, the Rambam titles the mitzvah, "*lilmod Torah*," which would normally translate to "Learn Torah," but then he immediately discusses a father's duty to teach Torah to his son. Logically, the Rambam should have first described the father's need to understand the Torah himself. Since it is quite unusual for the Rambam to present his material in a disorganized fashion, I suggest revising the translation of the Rambam's title: Instead of translating "*lilmod*" to "learn," I suggest revisiting the original meaning of the root. "*Lamed*" is the name of the letter that means "to," which describes both an action and an attachment. For example, one could either use "*l'yisrael*" in a sentence to describe the action of going to Israel, or to connote possession (attachment) by a person named Israel (i.e., Israel's house, or, the house that belongs to Israel). Thus, "*lilmod Torah*" could be an instruction to attach one's self to the Torah, and to actively encourage others to do the same. In one word, we must *transmit*. Like passing the baton in a relay race, we must take hold of the Torah as firmly as possible, work through the various components and remember the content well enough to pass it on to others, so others will also hold it firmly and continue the process.

The Chofetz Chaim discusses the mitzvah to transmit Torah as the 14th item in his list of positives, and the *Chinuch* elaborates on it under mitzvah number 419.

וּלְמַדְתֶּם אֹתָם

"You shall study them"
(Deut. 5:1)

Let's Discuss Understanding Torah

The Rambam and the *Chinuch* derive the instruction to learn and know Torah from the verse, "You shall study them and take care to do them" (Deut. 5:1). But the first verse that the Rambam quotes in reference to transmitting Torah is, "You shall teach them to your sons to speak about them" (Deut. 11:19). This verse begins with the Hebrew term, "*v'leemad'tam*," the root of which is "*lamed*," emphasizing the idea of attachment and transmitting described above. Apparently wishing to emphasize a different aspect of this mitzvah without changing the Rambam's order of presentation, both the *Chinuch* and Chofetz Chaim quote a different verse first: "You shall teach them diligently to your children" (Deut. 6:7). They begin with that verse to emphasize the full extent of the endeavor of transmitting Torah: The endeavor must be diligent.

(In fact, the Chofetz Chaim omits mentioning the verse about studying (Deut. 5:1), relying instead on the verse about teaching diligently (Deut. 6:7), since, in order to teach, one must first learn.)

Building on the emphasis on diligence, the Chofetz Chaim declares that the requirement is not just to learn the Torah, but to know it thoroughly and clearly. Since parents must teach the Torah to every child, everyone, not just rabbis and scholars, must know the Torah, and know it well. Everyone must understand the Torah to the best of his ability.

We Do This All the Time!

Of course, every time we sit down to learn, we do not need a reminder that we are performing a mitzvah. Still, if we train ourselves to be aware that we need to thoroughly understand the Torah, our concentration and patience should improve. We will be less satisfied with just "putting in the time," and we will collect reward miles immediately!

When reviewing homework assignments or parsha sheets with our children, we often discover new Torah tidbits that we had forgotten or never learned. Many times, it's the young, fresh perspective of the child that prompts the discovery. If we express pleasure in discovering the new information, our children will respond with equal or greater enthusiasm. By engendering greater excitement for Torah in our children, we garner more immediate reward miles.

Every encounter we have with the words of the Torah is an opportunity to clarify our thinking and extend our range of knowledge. When we ask our Rav for halachic advice, and then follow it up with more detailed questions, we are not just determining the proper course of action but discovering the nuances of the halacha. If we discover new things about Torah, we enhance our understanding of it. While we enhance our understanding, we should be conscious of fulfilling the mitzvah!

Just as the pursuit of Torah knowledge affects how we communicate with our rabbis, so should it influence the conversations we have with each other. Many Torah issues—including people's social roles and how people view their property—are people issues. When we converse with our friends and steer the discussion away from inconsequential matters (the weather, sport scores, etc.), we are bound to discover new truths. Even when an attempt to discuss matters of consequence fails, the attempt itself will foster dignity and self-esteem, particularly when coupled with consciousness of the mitzvah. We might even acquire another distinctive reward mile, namely, living up to the words of King David, "Oh, how I love Your Torah, all day long I speak of it" (Psalms 119:97).

וּפֶן־יָסוּרוּ מִלְּבָבְךָ

"... lest they depart from your heart"
(Deut. 4:9)

Let's Discuss Memorizing Torah

When we learn Torah, we should review material we have already learned to keep from forgetting it. This advice comes from the verse, "Lest they depart from your heart all the days of your life" (Deut. 4:9), which warns against the sin of forgetting. (Forgetting is sinful because it shows a lack of appreciation for Torah and because it allows our achievements to go to waste.)

The Sages further explain that even if someone masters the Torah at one time, he will probably forget things, so he must continue studying for the rest of his life, right up to the day he dies. To continuously learn and memorize Torah is to be constantly, or at least regularly, engaged in Torah study.

We Do This All the Time!

No student, while taking the time to review the new material he is learning, needs a reminder to be conscious of the Torah-study mitzvah; if he wasn't conscious of the mitzvah, he wouldn't be doing the studying. He might need a reminder to set aside the review time, but that would be a discussion for a different book. He also might need a reminder to be conscious when he is performing what he might consider an unrelated task, i.e., reviewing his children's homework assignments. Parents are qualified to review their children's homework because they know the information so much better than the children do; when parents review their children's homework, they might not feel that they are learning anything, but they are! They may have mastered the information at one time, but they still need to review. According to the verse, reviewing the material is a valid performance of the mitzvah. Keeping the mitzvah in mind might even help parents discover new insights into material that they might otherwise treat as uninteresting. Parents may also wish to remind their sons when they are studying for yeshiva high school exams to not only focus on the grade, but on the mitzvah as well. This may bring the immediate reward of tempering the pressure the student might feel, and also engender a warmer family atmosphere.

It is a rabbinic instruction to read through the weekly *sedrah*, twice in the Hebrew and once in the "*targum*." (Some people use Onkelos, some use Rashi and some use English.) After a few years of doing this, the activity can become mindless. Staying conscious of the requirement to remember the Torah, especially the words of the Creator of the Universe in the original Hebrew, can lend a fresh excitement to the activity.

We have a separate mitzvah to recite the three paragraphs of *Shema Yisrael* in the morning and in the evening. During these recitations, we should remember that the Torah is the source for each of the three paragraphs of the *Shema* (Deut. 6:4-9, Deut. 11:13-21 and Num. 15:37-41). Performing two mitzvos at the same time, such as reciting the *Shema* and reviewing Torah, is perfectly permissible (as long as neither takes away from the other). In this case, it is even better because the mitzvah of reviewing the Torah will augment the mitzvah of reciting the Shema: We will focus better on the Shema's implications because we are conscious of the need for constantly reviewing Torah passages.

וְהָגִיתָ בּוֹ יוֹמָם וָלַיְלָה

"You shall think about it day and night"
(Joshua 1:8)

Let's Discuss Scheduling Torah Study

Of course, not everyone is able to achieve Torah mastery or even remember the parts of Torah that they have learned, but everyone should try. The verse, "You shall think about it day and night" (Joshua 1:8), implies the instruction to set aside fixed times daily, at least once during the day and once at night, to study Torah. This instruction applies even to those who have already mastered the Torah, and so is especially applicable to those who are not yet masters.

The focus of the instruction to set time aside for study is on keeping a schedule, rather than on learning, understanding or remembering. That is, no minimum time requirement seems to exist; daily study can be relatively brief. The only obligation is to schedule some daytime learning and some evening-time learning. Accordingly, sessions could run an hour each morning and fifteen minutes each evening, or the reverse. The start times may vary according to the day of the week. For example, Monday and Thursday sessions could start fifteen minutes later to accommodate the longer morning services on those days. Alternatively, the start time could vary according to an event. For example, in the evenings, it could start right after Maariv (which varies with the time of sunset). The scheduled length of the session could vary. For example, the session could last for a half hour every day, except Friday when it stops after fifteen minutes to allow time to prepare for Shabbos. (Incidentally, Shabbos should also have a fixed schedule for learning day and night.)

Further, the subject matter could change between the day sessions and the evening sessions, and/or from day to day. For example, we might devote every morning to studying halacha, except Friday morning, which we might spend reading a parsha sheet.

The main message we should infer from the above examples is the core of the instruction: Make an inviolable commitment to Torah study. Torah study need not and should not become a tiresome burden. On the contrary, Torah study time should be non-negotiable personal time.

We Do This All the Time!

Many already have regular Torah study sessions, and plan on (or dream of) having more. However, the constant distractions (media, the phone, work, the kids, the community, family *simchas*) often make keeping a schedule impossible. Nevertheless, remembering that the Almighty requires us to have a schedule (albeit, in some cases, a brief one) could afford even the busiest Jew the fortitude to persevere.

Busy people might feel even better knowing that the study time they schedule for the mitzvah does not need to include all of the time that they intend to spend studying. No matter how hectic a day gets, we can always (barring extreme emergencies, of course) manage to learn for fifteen minutes at a certain time, even if it means we can only learn with our *chavrusa* over the phone. Those fifteen minutes could be our non-negotiable time for Torah study. While normally we might arrange with our *chavrusa* to learn an hour at that time and maintain that commitment whenever possible, nevertheless, when the inevitable hectic day occurs and the complete hour of learning becomes impossible, we could still persevere with our inviolable fifteen minutes and be satisfied that we have kept the mitzvah.

Commitments define a person's character. To be able to establish a lifelong habit of doing a good deed is a badge of honor. And it's that much more honorable if the good deed is regular Torah study, which is equated with all other good deeds. The reward miles for regular Torah study are benefits above and beyond that honor.

וְשִׁנַּנְתָּם לְבָנֶיךָ

"You shall teach them diligently to your children (students)" (Deut. 6:7)

Let's Discuss Teaching Torah

In addition to the verses that focus on learning, a number of verses guide the teaching of Torah. "You shall transmit them to your sons to speak of them" (Deut. 11:19) establishes a father's duty to teach his son as the highest priority. If, for whatever reason, the father is unable to teach his son, then he must hire someone to do it. The verse, "You shall make them known to your sons and grandsons" (Deut. 4:9), makes teaching Torah to one's grandson the second highest priority. After satisfying our family priorities, we must teach anyone who wants to learn from us: "You shall teach them diligently to your children" (Deut. 6:7). In that verse, "children" includes "students" as well.

We Do This All the Time!

Many of us already exert effort to transmit Torah. To fully appreciate each accomplishment, we should maintain awareness while making these efforts. For example, when we sign a tuition check for our child's Jewish education, we are fulfilling our highest duty: transmitting the Torah to the next generation. We should remember our role in maintaining the unbroken chain back to Sinai. The tuition checks will remain as high as before but the mitzvah consciousness will lighten the burden by highlighting the bargain we are receiving—an immediate reward mile.

The *Chinuch* quotes the Sages, who explain that transmitting Torah to the next generation begins as soon as parents teach their children to talk. Teaching a child to talk is the time to begin teaching Torah, because speech is a component, or at least a prerequisite, of Torah communication.

According to my rebbi, Rav Yaakov Weinberg, *zt"l*, the Sages revealed a profound secret about early childhood education: The first words parents teach a child should be the verse, "*Torah tziva lanu* ..." ("Moshe commanded us the Torah, it is a heritage of the community of Jacob"—Deut. 33:4), and then the verse, "*Shema Yisrael* ..." ("Understand Israel that G-d is our Lord, G-d is One"—Deut. 6:4). After those verses, children should learn other verses, until the age of six or seven, when they should start school.

Rav Weinberg pointed out that although the Sages were particular about the first two verses, and the order in which parents should teach those verses, they did not specify which verses parents should teach after those first two. Rav Weinberg also pointed out that a child just learning to speak obviously would not understand anything about the concepts contained in those verses. Therefore, Rav Weinberg concluded, the Sages must have been aware of a special, latent benefit of learning those two verses in just that order.

The Sages were revealing that to ensure a child's later development, to strengthen his ability to form a relationship with the Creator, a parent should teach him these verses in the proper order. Accordingly, we should follow the Sages' advice, even when it might be easier or more natural to first teach our children other phrases. Who knows what child-rearing problems we might avoid by diligently implanting these holy words within our child's psyche? We should trust in the wisdom of the Sages, whose authority came from Sinai. By transmitting the Sages' teachings, we can be confident that we have done the best for our children.

The requirement to teach extends to teaching adults. A famous saying of the Sages is, "I learned much from teachers, more from my peers, and the most from my students." How is it possible to learn from those who know less? It is possible because when someone challenges our opinions, it can often give us a new perspective; when a student is confused about a lesson, his teacher is forced to develop greater clarity in order to explain the material. Sometimes, we might refrain from asking questions because we do not wish to bother our teacher. To find the courage to speak up, we should remember the teaching aspect of the mitzvah and the subsequent reward miles.

Postscript: WHY WE DON'T HAVE WOMEN KOLLELS

Jewish women are exempt from the mitzvah of transmitting Torah. Many perceive this exemption as discriminatory, particularly in light of the *Chinuch's* statement that one best develops his relationship with G-d by knowing the Torah. It is beyond the scope of this work to fully explain why this exemption does not discriminate against women. However, the subject is worth exploring, if only because it is inconceivable that the *Chinuch* would not consider a relationship with G-d a primary goal for women.

Instead of questioning Torah concepts, we should accept them as insights and determine which theories we might build from them. This is similar to the scientific method, by which scientists collect sets of facts and seek to build theories that explain them. The Torah teaches that everyone must develop a relationship with G-d, and further, that men, but not women, must engage in Torah scholarship. The conclusion should be that to form a relationship with G-d, men need special guidance or tools that women do not need. This conclusion agrees with the observation that women are generally more adept at forming relationships with others. By explaining that men need Torah scholarship to form a relationship with G-d, the *Chinuch* might just be addressing the extra prodding that men require over women to form any relationship. Quite possibly, implies the *Chinuch*, without Torah scholarship, a man's relationship to G-d would be as limited as that of a pet to its master.

Although they are exempt from the mitzvah of transmitting the Torah, women still need to learn Torah, a need that stems from their obligation to properly perform their mitzvos. A woman must learn a great deal of Torah just to perform the mitzvos of keeping kosher, Shabbos and family purity, the responsibilities that are primarily hers. So why is an instruction necessary for learning Torah? Why must we be instructed to read the instructions?

To answer this, perhaps we should distinguish between Torah scholarship of theory and scholarship of practical knowledge of the Torah. By "practical," I mean knowledge of the details that we must understand to perform each mitzvah. By "theory," I mean everything in the Torah *besides* the details of the mitzvos. Of course, to learn the theory we must first learn the practical aspects of the mitzvos. However, the reverse is not true. The mitzvah to transmit Torah has as its ultimate goal the scholarship of theory.

An example might more easily clarify the distinction between theory and practice: Consider the mitzvah to honor elders and Torah scholars. Practical knowledge of this mitzvah includes learning to stand in the presence of an elder or Torah scholar. Women must learn that, and they do not need a separate mitzvah (transmitting Torah) to learn it. On the other hand, the mitzvah of honoring elders does not include the requirement to study that mitzvah's theory (i.e., why the two types of people, elders and Torah scholars, are treated the same way). To make sure we learn the theory, rather than just the practical application, the Torah includes the separate mitzvah of transmitting the Torah.

Again, we might build a theory from the facts that the Torah presents. The Torah states that only men need to learn, retain and teach the Torah's theoretical concepts, but women do not need to, although they can if they wish. This distinction might support the theory that men are more theoretically oriented, while women, in general, are more practical. This theory could give us insight into some of the many differences between men and women, and why we don't have women kollels.

PUT IT INTO ACTION!

Have in mind the mitzvah of "Transmit Torah" when:

- You clarify a halacha with the Rav (the aspect of understanding Torah).
- You try to turn the discussion away from trivia toward Torah issues (the aspect of understanding Torah).

- You listen to Torah tapes (the aspect of understanding Torah). If this is a regular time such as driving to and from work, then also the aspect of setting times for Torah study. If you've already listened to that particular tape before, then also the aspect of not forgetting.
- You review Torah learning (the aspects of understanding Torah and not forgetting).
- You listen to a speaker, and he ends up talking about an idea that we already know (the aspects of understanding Torah and not forgetting).
- You read the weekly parsha as the Sages have instructed—twice in the original, once in the translation (the aspects of understanding Torah and not forgetting).
- You say Shema morning and evening, and you contemplate the deeper meaning of the words (the aspects of understanding Torah and setting times).
- You attend a regular shiur or learn with your chavrusa (the aspects of understanding Torah and setting times).
- You review homework with your children (the aspect of teaching Torah).
- You coach your children on making brachos (the aspect of teaching Torah).
- You take care of paying your children's yeshiva tuition (the aspect of teaching Torah).
- You learn with a chavrusa who is weaker than you (the aspect of teaching Torah).

Notes and Observations

אַל־תִּפְנוּ אֶל־הָאֱלִילִם

“Do not turn to idols”
(Lev. 19:4)

Don’t Read Junk

We can always find excuses for engaging in other activities at the expense of Torah learning. We can even excuse our leisure time, excessive as it is by historical standards, by claiming that it’s impossible for us to function without it. However, considering the all-encompassing mandate to learn G-d’s truth through Torah scholarship, how could we possibly excuse the very antithesis of Torah learning—the study of material opposed to the truth?

The Basic Instruction

According to the Sages, the Torah instruction, “Do not turn to idols” (Lev. 19:4), warns against researching idol worship (e.g., its practices and concepts). The Chofetz Chaim presents this concept as the 16th in his list of negatives, and the *Chinuch* discusses it under mitzvah number 213.

Let’s Discuss

Idol worship is such a foreign concept to most of us that we would expect minimal opportunity for reward miles, given the absence of opportunity and motivation to engage in this prohibited practice.

However, the *Chinuch* explains that, in addition to the study of idol worship practices and concepts, the mitzvah also prohibits the study or perusal of any material that would lead a person to question any Torah concept.

The *Chinuch*'s definition makes this mitzvah relevant because everyone today must contend with a profusion of information antithetical to Torah values. Unfortunately, this mitzvah instruction will not be very compelling to someone who is already interested in a field of study that is foreign to Torah values (e.g., Bible criticism). Such a person has, by definition, rejected the authority of the Torah. However, the Torah has not rejected him, so we should not reject him, either. We should try our best to assist him in discovering the falseness of the premise on which his field of study stands.

The mitzvah is more relevant to those fully aware and committed to the truth of the Torah. However, curiosity sometimes entices even observant Jews to explore. The mitzvah not to study idolatry advises against such curiosity; it is a waste of time and a dangerous diversion. Further, the Sages caution, we must not engage in debate to prove the Torah's validity, unless we are trying to rescue other Jews from thinking that is opposed to Torah. In such situations, we must only engage under the direction of a Torah scholar.

We Often Avoid This

Every time we skip reading the horoscopes or turn the radio dial away from the inane musings of some media celebrity on the meaning of life, we are protecting ourselves from perusing material that is contrary to the Torah. By remembering that our distaste for such content is ultimately rooted in our connection to the mitzvah of not studying idolatry, we will earn reward miles to Heaven and refresh our commitment to the Torah.

PUT IT INTO ACTION!

Have in mind the mitzvah of "Don't Read Junk" when:

- You ignore horoscopes and similar foolishness.
- You change radio stations to avoid listening to pieces that are contrary to Torah.

Notes and Observations

הָקֵם תָּקִים עִמּוֹ

"You shall surely help him lift them up"
(Deut. 22:4)

Give a Lift

The Basic Instruction

If you cross paths with someone who needs help loading a burden onto his beast, the Torah states, "you shall surely help him lift them up" (Deut. 22:4). According to the Sages, the instruction describes the obligation we have to help another person load a burden, whether it be onto a pack animal or onto the person's own back. The Chofetz Chaim discusses this instruction as the 71st in his list of positives, while the *Chinuch* discusses it under mitzvah number 541.

Let's Discuss

According to the *Chinuch*, the mitzvah only applies when someone *needs help* loading up. For example, we are not obligated to help delivery people who are doing their jobs; it would be extremely difficult for us to live normal lives if we stopped to lend a hand every time we saw a delivery person. It would also come as quite a shock to the delivery person. Although some people might protest that the world would be wonderful if everyone stopped to help each other, it is important to remember two things: First, people enjoy accomplishing things themselves.

Second, if everybody stopped to help delivery people, the importance of their jobs would be diminished, their employers would not value them as much and they would not be able to earn a living. Therefore, it makes sense that the mitzvah only applies when the necessary manpower is missing.

The mitzvah to "help him lift them up" comes with conditions: According to both the Chofetz Chaim and the *Chinuch*, we are excused from helping if the owner of the burden is not willing to pay for the help; that is, we are entitled to seek fair compensation for our effort. Also, we are exempt if it is beneath our dignity to engage in the effort required. For example, a woman may feel it is beneath her dignity to help someone change a tire. If we are unsure whether or not we can claim this exemption, we should ask ourselves whether we would engage in the effort if it were our own burden. If the answer is no, then we are exempt. (Presumably, we could also claim exemption due to other conditions, such as a sore back. That is, if I would not attempt the effort on my own behalf because of a sore back, then I am exempt, as long as my back is sore, from helping someone else.) However, according to the Sages, anyone who recognizes the plight of his fellow and puts aside his own dignity, and/or forgoes his right to compensation, brings a blessing upon himself.

We Do This All the Time!

While the need to load a beast of burden has become rare, cars and trucks are modern-day stand-ins. During snowstorms, people often help push other people's cars that are stuck in the snow. Even though our motivation may be simply to clear the road to get our own car through, we are still engaging in a mitzvah. To ensure our reward, we should be particularly careful to keep the mitzvah in mind, because our self-serving motives could potentially eclipse the mitzvah. Pushing a car out of our path is comparable to performing the mitzvah of eating on Shabbos. We eat because we are hungry, but if we remember that eating on Shabbos is a mitzvah, we earn reward. Freeing cars that are stuck in the snow may provide an added bonus: Our awareness that we are acting in accordance with the Almighty's instruction will surely subdue the frustration and discomfort associated with the task.

A similar example of the mitzvah to help another person with his burden is stopping to help someone with a flat tire or a stalled car. Even when the only help we can offer is the use of a cell phone to call a tow truck, we are fulfilling a mitzvah. In fact, in dangerous neighborhoods, simply offering to call for help is the preferred method of fulfilling the mitzvah because we are not allowed to put ourselves in danger, even when someone else appears to be in danger.

Moving day, the modern version of a barn-raising, is another opportunity to fulfill the mitzvah. (In pioneer days, a barn-raising would happen in one day when all of the neighboring farmers would convene to help a newcomer get established.) These days, young couples often have to move to bigger houses or apartments to accommodate their growing families, and on moving day, all of their friends might convene to help load up the moving van. It is a wonderful act of friendship that becomes even more meaningful when the participants remember that they are not only cementing a friendship, but also engaging in a Divine act.

Perhaps the most common example of fulfilling the mitzvah is when we help load the car with packages (groceries, etc.) that our spouse has purchased. Naturally, we help out of love and because of the mutual understanding that we have developed with our spouse. That relationship is wonderfully enhanced when we remind ourselves that we are not only building our personal relationship but also infusing the relationship with a Divine quality by following an instruction from the Almighty.

The mitzvah can also apply to someone meeting an arrival (even a spouse) at the airport, train station or bus depot, and helping him or her carry the bags to the car, especially if the traveler has too many to carry alone. We could also fulfill the mitzvah by opening the door for someone who is carrying packages. When we help others carry burdens, we should keep the mitzvah in mind to receive the full reward, and to reinforce our alignment with the Almighty's will.

My final example of helping with a vehicle explains why I titled this section, "Give a Lift." Surely, helping someone transport himself is as important as helping him transport his goods. People give each other lifts all the time, and the mitzvah to "give a lift" is what inspires them! Whenever we have a passenger in the car, we should remember how such assistance conforms to the Almighty's will. The road miles become reward miles to Heaven!

PUT IT INTO ACTION!

Have in mind the mitzvah of "Give a Lift" when:

- You pick up someone who needs a ride.
- You see someone with car trouble and either help directly or call for assistance.
- You help serve at meal time.

Notes and Observations

DAY 23

עָזֹב תַּעֲזֹב עִמּוֹ

"You shall surely help him" (Exod. 23:5)

וְהִתְעַלַּמְתָּ מֵהֶם

"and [do not] hide yourself from them" (Deut. 22:4)

Relieve Everyone; Don't Pass Up an Opportunity

The Basic Instruction

Two mitzvos instruct us to help unload an animal or person whose load is unmanageable. These two mitzvos are clones of each other, differing only in how they are expressed (one positive and the other negative). That is, when we perform the positive mitzvah, we also avoid the negative; when we violate the negative mitzvah, we also ignore the positive.

I have named the positive mitzvah, "Relieve everyone," and its source is, "If you see the donkey of one whom you hate lying under its burden, would you hesitate to help him? Rather you shall surely help him" (Exod. 23:5). The Chofetz Chaim presents this as the 70th in his list of positives, and the *Chinuch* discusses it under mitzvah number 80.

I call the negative one, "Don't pass up an opportunity." Its source verse is, "You shall not see your brother's donkey or his ox fallen down by the way, and hide yourself from them" (Deut. 22:4). The Chofetz Chaim presents this as the 183rd in his list of negatives, and the *Chinuch* discusses it under mitzvah number 540.

According to the Sages, these two mitzvos instructing us to help unload an animal or person are very similar in concept to the mitzvah "Give a lift" presented previously. In the classical sources, these two mitzvos are called the "unloading" mitzvos because they discuss helping to unload, while "Give a lift" is called the "loading" mitzvah because it discusses helping to load up. The discussion below shows how the interplay among these three mitzvos provides Torah guidance on some complicated issues, such as the cost of helping someone, the reluctance to help strangers or opponents, and animal cruelty.

Let's Discuss

It is significant that Deuteronomy 22:4 is split in half to produce two mitzvos (first the negative mitzvah, "Don't pass up an opportunity," and then the positive mitzvah, "Give a lift"). Since "Don't pass up an opportunity" is a clone of "Relieve everyone" (discussed in the Torah many, many pages earlier), it is as if the two positive mitzvos of "Give a lift" and "Relieve everyone" appear in the same verse. With these literary devices of positive and negative statements invoking past issues, the Torah echoes the real world, where helping people properly can require weighing a number of complex factors. Indeed, both the Chofetz Chaim and the *Chinuch* refer their readers from one mitzvah to the other, encouraging the reader to discover all of the details that the two positive mitzvos share, yet still discern why they are separate.

The instructions for the two activities of loading and unloading are alike in that we are exempt from helping when the task required is beneath our dignity. For example, should someone want a rabbi, especially one dressed like a rabbi, to load up a pack animal or unpack an overburdened animal, the rabbi may decline to help because of the disrespect such a task could bring his office. On the other hand, the two activities differ in regard to compensation. When performing the mitzvah, "Relieve everyone," by helping to unload an overburdened animal, we may not ask for compensation; when performing, "Give a lift," on the other hand, by helping to load a pack animal, we may first insist on compensation.

By recognizing the difference between being in need and being in pain, we can understand why, in this respect, these two rules diverge. A person or animal struggling under a load is in pain; the Torah instructs us to be sensitive to that pain. We cannot develop that sensitivity if we demand payment. However, losing our dignity is also painful; we should not have to endure pain in order to relieve someone else's pain. That is why someone with a sore back is exempt from the mitzvah "to help him lift them up." Halachic commentators may have chosen the loss of dignity as their example of the passerby's pain because loss of dignity is the least obvious form of pain. They probably wanted to sensitize their readers to the very real quality of emotional pain.

By contrast, when a person wishes to load up, he appears to have a need. He can prove his need by willingly paying fair compensation for the help that he seeks. (If he has no money to give, then he needs charity rather than help, which calls for a different mitzvah; I discuss that mitzvah later.) Once he has proven his need, the passerby is obligated to help. However, if the task results in physical pain to the passerby, or in the passerby's loss of dignity, the compensation may be inadequate. Whether or not the task could result in the passerby's pain or loss of dignity is up to the passerby to decide. Therefore, a useful balance comes into play: The person in need of help decides how much he is willing to pay for the help, and the passerby decides how little he is prepared to earn for the effort.

The preceding distinction between people in pain and people in need might help explain why the Torah provides two separate positive mitzvos that both prescribe the same concept: Lend a helping hand. The mitzvah in this chapter, "Relieve everyone," introduces an extra measure of care for the special case of people in pain. People in pain deserve other people's unconditional attention and effort. The verse seems to suggest that animals in pain deserve the same care. Interestingly, the *Chinuch* does not mention the pain of animals in his discussion of the mitzvah, although he certainly mentions it in his discussions of other mitzvos.

The Chofetz Chaim does mention the animal's pain, and uses it to explain several rules. For example, one rule states that the "Don't pass up an opportunity" mitzvah applies even when the animal's owner appears to be at fault for overburdening the animal. Moreover, if, after unloading the animal, the owner reloads the animal, perhaps with the help of the passerby, and the animal falls again, the mitzvah continues to apply: The passerby must help unload the animal the second time. Even if the animal falls one hundred times, the passerby must continue to help because the verse states, "you shall surely help him," implying that the passerby must help as much as necessary. In fact, the mitzvah includes a duty to accompany the owner and animal for some distance (unless the owner states that it is not necessary) to ensure that the animal does not fall again. If the passerby does accompany the driver and animal, or gives any other additional help, he may request compensation; requesting compensation is only forbidden when it comes to the specific act of unloading the burden.

To fully underscore the concern we must have for the animal's pain, the Chofetz Chaim rules that if two opportunities arise simultaneously (one to help load and the other to help unload), the latter takes precedence because it relieves both the driver and the animal.

We Do This All the Time!

Some people have pets and are very solicitous of their welfare. Whenever they are ensuring that no harm comes to their pets, pet owners are performing a mitzvah, and they should keep the mitzvah in mind. They should also keep in mind that this lesson from the mitzvah, "Don't pass up an opportunity," has some limits: It is not a mitzvah to treat animals like people. If we have a choice between the welfare of any moral human being and the welfare of an animal, we must make the human our top priority. The *Chinuch* explains (during a discussion of his concern for animals, in the context of a different mitzvah) that the concern we must show animals will awaken and develop our skills of compassion, which we can in turn extend to our fellow man.

Sometimes, even people who don't own pets encounter an animal in pain. It may be an animal that got hit by a car or stuck in a narrow opening, or it might just be a stray cat mewing at the door. Whatever we do to offer the animal relief is fulfillment of a mitzvah. Often, we might be nervous about getting close to a strange animal because the animal could be diseased or vicious. The Torah teaches that we should not put ourselves in danger; in questionable circumstances, we might be better off calling the proper authorities. Nevertheless, even calling the authorities is a mitzvah because we have avoided ignoring the animal's pain.

Let's Discuss "Hate" (Version 1)

The verse for the mitzvah, "Relieve everyone," starts with, "If you see the donkey of one whom you hate lying under its burden ..."

(Exod. 23:5). Who is the "one whom you hate"? The *Chinuch* explains it simply: He is a person that someone just doesn't like. The Torah is opposed to feelings of ill will among members of the community, and says that this mitzvah is an opportunity to overcome those feelings. Accordingly, should we simultaneously encounter two opportunities to perform the mitzvah of unloading, one for a friend or stranger and the other for someone we dislike, we should first help the person we dislike. We will then reap the additional reward associated with overcoming ill will.

We Do This All the Time!

It is not uncommon to attempt to diminish ill will. Sometimes, a co-worker, a person in our social circle or even a family member just rubs us the wrong way. In response, we often resolve to do our best to remain courteous rather than let the tension escalate; letting the tension escalate would be uncomfortable because we still have to see the person we dislike on a frequent basis. Every time we treat the person we dislike with courtesy, we should remember that such conduct is in concert with the Torah. We will gain reward for the mitzvah and develop self-confidence for being on the right course.

We Can Do Even Better

The Torah instructs us to choose to help those we dislike. If we do help, we might just find ourselves cementing new friendships. I can attest to this personally. Once, I got a job that I was very happy to have secured. It paid significantly more than my old job had, and I felt certain that I could learn a great deal from my new boss. The fly in the ointment was the senior secretary who ran the office. I found her personality quite offensive; she seemed to criticize and belittle everyone's efforts while maintaining an exalted regard for her own. My co-workers also had trouble getting along with her. Because I realized that I could not avoid dealing with her on a regular basis, I resolved to change the relationship. I went out of my way to do her favors: If I was getting coffee, I would offer to get her a cup. If we were both waiting for the photocopier, I would let her go first, explaining that I knew she was busier than I. And so on. I maintained an attitude that was neither servile nor sarcastic, an attitude derived from the genuine desire to improve the relationship. Within a month, the secretary's manner softened, I started to appreciate the great pressure of her job and our relationship greatly improved!

From this experience and others, I have become quite convinced that this Torah insight on behavior modification will work for anyone who has to spend significant time with someone he doesn't like. Overcoming such differences only requires one party to choose to help the other, and to be consciously driven to stop disliking that person. One can gain instant reward miles from consciously adhering to this mitzvah.

Let's Discuss "Hate" (Version 2)

Although the *Chinuch* says that "hate" in the phrase, "one whom you hate," means "dislike," he states that "one whom you dislike" is only the secondary meaning of the phrase. The Chofetz Chaim quotes the primary meaning.

According to the Chofetz Chaim, the Torah is primarily referring to someone whom one *should* hate, and therefore keep at a distance. A Jew should distance himself from a person who defies Torah law. Today, most of us cannot avoid interacting with community and family members who violate Torah laws, but usually, these violators are not defiant of the Torah; rather, they simply are not yet inspired by it. However, some do blatantly defy Torah law. Consider the example of a single witness who sees someone stealing a pen and cautions the thief not to go through with the theft, but finds himself ignored. That solitary witness cannot testify in Jewish court because the court requires at least two valid witnesses for a testimony. If the witness publicizes the crime by testifying, he is guilty of *lashon hara* (gossip), even though he knows that not only is he telling the truth but that he tried to prevent the theft. In such a situation, the Torah instructs the witness to remain silent but bear hatred for the thief by keeping a distance from him. (This obligation only exists when the wrongdoer acknowledges that he is acting illegally but persists in doing so.)

The instruction to maintain a distance comes with a condition: When the witness, who must normally keep his distance, finds the unethical person (who has never made any effort to correct his wrongdoing) or the unethical person's animal struggling under a load, the witness must help because the wrongdoer is still a member of the community. The witness is only exempt from the obligation to help if the crime he witnessed was severe enough (e.g., "mob" activity) to classify the perpetrator as a totally immoral person outside the norms of the community. However, after providing the assistance, the witness must again distance himself from the perpetrator.

Perhaps the most profound reward mile presented in this book emerges from the instructions to the type of witness I described above. Rav A. Henoch Leibowitz discusses the difficulty of those instructions in his book, *Majesty of Man*. The witness must create distance between himself and the thief, then override that distance to help the thief, and then recreate the distance. The witness's predicament is extraordinarily frustrating and he may well bemoan the Almighty's decision not to provide him with a second witness. If he feels that way, he should remind himself that the Almighty is properly governing the world and will ensure that justice is served; the witness's job is simply to follow His instructions.

If the thief later requires help from the sole witness (with a pack animal or otherwise), that witness, the one person who knows that the thief is a criminal, may wonder why the Almighty would arrange such a meeting. After all, for the two to meet again under such circumstances must be a Divine act! The answer comes from a phrase fifteen verses after the phrase that led to this discussion of "the donkey of one whom you hate." G-d promises, "Behold, I will send an angel before you to guard you on the way …" (Exod. 23:20). Rashi explains that G-d is describing how He will maintain His connection with the Jewish people if they distance themselves by sinning. Instead of appearing Himself, G-d will send an angel. In *Darash Moshe*, Rav Moshe Feinstein, *zt"l*, further explains that when people sin, G-d's personal presence would overwhelm and destroy them. Therefore, G-d, rather than protecting the Jews Himself, sends an angel to protect them.

Is any reward mile more profound than this one? Consider the scenario more closely: The witness alone knows the thief's crime. Because the witness has criticized the thief, the thief knows that the witness knows. Now the thief needs the help of the one person who is least likely to want to help him. By helping, the witness lets the guilty party taste the benefits of belonging to the community. By immediately re-distancing himself, he makes it clear that the guilty party cannot receive full benefits until he has corrected his faults. By following Torah instructions, the witness's reward is that he has become like an angel, a personal messenger of G-d!

In summary, the phrase, "one whom you hate," adds another element to the mitzvos about helping people—the need to overcome feelings of ill will toward others, and to harbor at least a minimum level of compassion for everyone, even for those we should normally keep at a distance.

We Can Do Even Better

It is relatively rare for someone to witness an unethical act. However, it is unfortunately not that uncommon for a community to learn that one of its members has been convicted of an unethical act. For example, let's say a member of one's community is convicted of embezzling a large sum of money. He is sent to prison for a few years and all of his assets are seized. After his release from prison, he may choose to return to his community but find himself in need of a job and a place to live. If we help him, we fulfill not only the mitzvah of charity but also the mitzvah of providing help even to someone with a blemished past. We might feel uncomfortable and ambiguous about our dealings with such a person, about whether or not we should help him. Maintaining awareness of these mitzvos will help us act with assurance.

We might also deem it proper to keep our distance from those who, though not necessarily convicted by the courts, are known to abuse their spouses or children, refuse to grant their spouses a divorce agreement (a "get"), refuse to appear before a Jewish court, are notorious for not paying their debts or have engaged in similar unethical acts, provided we know about their behavior from personal experience rather than from hearsay. Although the concept of keeping distant from someone who acts immorally was developed in conjunction with the mitzvah "Relieve everyone," the mitzvah to keep in mind when keeping distant is, "Do not pity the immoral."

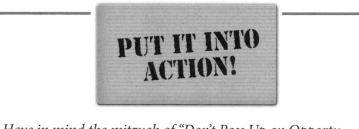

PUT IT INTO ACTION!

Have in mind the mitzvah of "Don't Pass Up an Opportunity" when:

- You choose to work with someone you don't like, with the hope of improving the relationship.
- You decide to care for an injured animal (for example, by calling the ASPCA) or recognize a lost pet and notify the owner.

Notes and Observations

וְלֹא תִקְפֹּץ אֶת־יָדְךָ מֵאָחִיךָ הָאֶבְיוֹן
כִּי־פָתֹחַ תִּפְתַּח אֶת־יָדְךָ

"You shall not ... shut your hand from your needy brother. Rather, you shall surely open your hand to him." (Deut. 15:7-8)

Give Charity; Don't Be a Tightwad

The Basic Instruction

The Torah states, "you shall not harden your heart nor shut your hand from your needy brother" (Deut. 15:7), and continues, "Rather you shall surely open your hand to him" (Deut. 15:8). From the latter verse comes the instruction to give charity; from the former comes the prohibition against being tight-fisted and refusing to give charity. These two mitzvos are mirror images of each other, different only in how they are expressed (one positive and the other negative). That is, when we perform the positive mitzvah, we thereby avoid the negative; when we violate the negative mitzvah, we thereby ignore the positive.

The Chofetz Chaim elaborates on these mitzvos as the 38th positive and 62nd negative, in their respective lists. The *Chinuch* discusses them in the order that they appear in the Torah; the negative is mitzvah number 478 and the positive is mitzvah number 479.

Let's Discuss

The Chofetz Chaim points out that the instruction to give charity applies even if the same needy person requires our donations again and again. Furthermore, one's charity should extend even to needy non-Jews, provided those non-Jews are moral (i.e., they observe the seven Noahide laws).

The ideal charitable gift is the full amount that the poor person is lacking, as defined by the poor person's station in life. (For example, a delivery person whose vehicle stops working cannot earn a living because he lacks a working vehicle. However, his station in life does not command a new, top-of-the-line vehicle; a repair to the existing vehicle should suffice.) On the other hand, the donor is limited to a maximum gift of 20% of his own annual income. If the pauper's needs exceed that amount, then the donor should contribute the amount remaining in his 20% budget. For example, if the donor earns $100,000 annually, he should not give more than $20,000 annually to charity. Thus, if the pauper needs $2,000 to repair the vehicle's transmission and the willing donor has already donated $19,000 to other charities that year, the donor should only give him $1,000.

If we are aware of several people in need of our charity, as is usually the case, then we should give first to our closest relative, and then, if funds are still available, to the next closest, and so on. For example, we would first attend to a needy person in our own household; we would attend to a needy person in our own city over a needy person in another city; we would help needy people in cities in Israel over needy people in cities outside of Israel.

The prohibition against refusing to give charity reminds us to respond to need in a warm and understanding fashion, even when we have nothing left to give. We should accompany all donations with a friendly smile and never with a scowl or a rebuke, even if the needy person has fallen on hard times because of his own irresponsibility. It is only fitting that we should be gracious because the Torah guarantees that no harm will come from giving charity, not even a shortness of funds. (The *Chinuch*, though, implies that a shortness of funds may occur, but will be more than offset by other blessings.) The Sages taught that one who gives and convinces others to give charity receives a greater reward than one who merely gives charity, presumably because the former benefits both the giver and the recipient.

The *Chinuch* points out that the best way to fulfill the charity mitzvah is through a properly administered charity fund. That way, both the donor and the recipient remain anonymous, thus preventing potential embarrassment. The *Chinuch* further points out that we can fulfill the charity mitzvah not only with money, but also with any resource that the needy person lacks, even if that resource is only friendship or a kind word. Therefore, even a rich person can be a worthy recipient of charity.

Sometimes, we know a person is needy but, to their credit, they refuse assistance. In such cases, we should employ deceit. For example, we could offer assistance in the form of a loan, and then neglect to seek repayment. However, people who are capable of helping themselves, but are too miserly to do so, are not entitled to charity. For example, people who take expensive vacations every year are not entitled to tuition assistance for their children's educations.

We Do This All the Time!

Charity is a hallmark of the Jewish people. It is so unnatural for a Jew to ignore the plights of others that some suggest investigating the genealogy of anyone who is not charitable to confirm that he is Jewish! Because generosity comes so naturally to us, we must be especially careful when giving charity to remember the mitzvah. To receive the full reward for our charity, we must remember our primary motivation: G-d's will. Keeping the mitzvah in mind will also help us conform to the details of the mitzvah.

We Can Do Even Better

Many times, our hearts are torn asunder when we learn about corrupt political situations, formidable natural disasters, implausible war-related calamities and so on, from newspapers, letters, emails and the like. Our natural compassion implores us to respond, and yet, the sheer volume of requests for help confounds us into frustration; sometimes, into inaction. To counter such paralysis, we should remember that the charity mitzvah provides minimum and maximum guidelines. Even though we would wish to solve all the misfortunes of the world, our duty is to act within the mitzvah's parameters. That reminder will provide us with the resolve and confidence to respond appropriately. (Where life and death are at stake, the following guidelines usually change.)

First, we must know our budget for charity donations. The optimum amount is 20% of one's income, but 10% is an acceptable amount. (Anyone who feels that he cannot afford 10% may be correct, but he should consult a qualified Rav to make sure.)

Next, we must ensure that we have met the needs of those closest to us before we address the needs of others. The saying, "Charity begins at home," originates in halacha. First, we should consider whether we have any family members that require assistance. In this category, we should include any of our older children, even if married, who are not yet self-supporting. Tuition payments and living expenses for children still at home may also count, although some authorities consider some of these expenses mandatory, and therefore, not charity. (The reader should consult his Rav.) Remember that the ideal charitable gift is the full amount that the needy person is lacking, as defined by his station in life. Even though it is we who may have made our children accustomed to a certain standard, it is still a charitable act to help them maintain that standard until they are capable of doing so on their own. However, we only need to give our children charity if they are emotionally distraught by not having the level of comfort that they previously enjoyed. By the same token, if any other family member has suffered a financial reversal and is now distraught over his reduced circumstances, he, too, should be a charity recipient.

After we have met the needs of our extended family, we should address the needs within our community. We should provide first for poor families without the basic necessities; then for Jewish schools because a Jewish education is a basic necessity. (If tuitions do not cover the school's expenses, then helping to support the school would be a way of providing the families that use the school with one of their basic necessities.) Next, we should consider young people in our community without jobs or employable skills. Any job we can offer them qualifies as the highest form of charity; a job not only provides basic necessities, but it does so on a perpetual basis. Thereafter, we should help to maintain other community members' lifestyles that those people can no longer afford. For example, we could give to a retirement center that accepts public support.

Donating to charity this way—proactively—demonstrates our conscious adherence to the precept of charity. We can rest assured that our compassion is deep and genuine because it conforms exactly to the Almighty's wishes.

PUT IT INTO ACTION!

Have in mind the mitzvah of "Give Charity, Don't Be a Tightwad" when:

- You recognize and prioritize solicitation letters.
- At the occasion of a family reunion, you learn of someone's financial difficulty and offer assistance, because you remember that the best allocation of charity funds is to those close to you.
- When working on the household budget, you separate a part for charity.

Notes and Observations

IT'S JUST GOOD BUSINESS

Many of the interactions we have with other people are business dealings. Because money is involved, business interactions might feel far removed from Heaven. But they're not. The Torah has quite a bit to say on the topic of business dealings. Our interactions in the business world give us many opportunities to earn reward miles to Heaven.

בְּיוֹמוֹ תִתֵּן שְׂכָרוֹ
וְלֹא־תָבוֹא עָלָיו הַשֶּׁמֶשׁ

"On his day you shall give him his wages; neither shall the sun go down on it ..." (Deut. 24:15)

Make the Payroll on Time; Don't Delay

The Basic Instruction

Two mitzvos instruct employers to pay wages in a timely manner. These two mitzvos are mirror images of each other, different only in how they are expressed (one positive and the other negative). That is, when we perform the positive mitzvah, we thereby avoid the negative; when we violate the negative mitzvah, we ignore the positive.

I have named the positive mitzvah, "Make the payroll on time," and its source is, "On his day you shall give him his wages" (Deut. 24:15). The Chofetz Chaim presents this as number 66 in his list of positives, and the *Chinuch* discusses it under mitzvah number 588.

I call the negative one, "Don't delay." It has two source verses, "the wages of a hired man shall not remain with you (all night) until the morning" (Lev. 19:13), and, "neither shall the sun go down on it" (Deut. 24:15). The Chofetz Chaim presents this as number 38 in his list of negatives, and the *Chinuch* discusses it under mitzvah number 230.

Let's Discuss

An employer must not withhold payment past the day or night during which the worker completed the work. The classic examples are a laborer who worked all day until the evening, and a laborer who worked all night until the next morning. The employer must pay the former that night, meaning before the next morning, and pay the latter that day, meaning before the next evening. These time frames come from the "Don't delay" Torah verses, "the wages of a hired man shall not remain with you (all night) until the morning" (Lev. 19:13), and, "neither shall the sun go down on it" (Deut. 24:15). The first verse refers to a day laborer, and the second to a night worker. An employer must pay a worker who finishes in the middle of the day or night by the end of that day or night.

The Chofetz Chaim points out that these mitzvos about wages protect not only Jewish workers, but non-Jewish workers, as well, provided those non-Jews follow the seven Noahide laws. (Torah law protects moral people, and by definition if non-Jews comply with the Noahide laws, they are moral people.) The *Chinuch* points out that the obligation to compensate promptly belongs to all employers, not just to employers of day laborers. At the end of any agreed-upon term, such as a week or a month, the employer must pay his employee by the end of the day (or night) during which his employee completed his work; it is a transgression to neglect to do so. The sources further explain that these mitzvos also apply to the employers of contractors and to the renters of any property other than land.

We Do This All the Time!

We fulfill these two mitzvos all the time. To earn full reward, we should maintain consciousness of it. In fact, we can receive reward for two mitzvos at the same time! For example, we pay the babysitter at the end of the evening, the cab driver at the end of the ride, the transit fare at the beginning of the ride (that qualifies, too) and the cleaner and the shoe repairman when we pick up our goods. We pay out of habit or necessity, but the opportunities to make those payments still offer us a chance to regularly connect with the Almighty as long as we maintain awareness that we are performing His will.

Most businesses have a regular payroll. An employer is usually careful about being timely because such efficiency keeps his workers happy and motivated. But he might not always make those payments with relish. Sometimes, he may even resent signing certain paychecks because he is not really satisfied with his employees' work. Remembering that issuing the payroll on time is a mitzvah will give him joy and satisfaction. The knowledge that he is obeying the Almighty will certainly encourage him to have a more distinguished approach to the regular task of signing checks. The mitzvah consciousness could also help him focus on solving his problems: Happily signing a paycheck for an employee with whom he is not satisfied may just engender within him the positive attitude he needs toward the employee to discover a way to correct the problem.

We have many other opportunities to perform the mitzvah of paying on time. Again, according to the *Chinuch*, the mitzvah applies to renters of property (unless the property is land). Paying bills in a timely fashion is a fulfillment of the mitzvah because we often pay bills for things that we are renting. For example, we often "rent" hot water heaters, furnaces and telephone equipment. We also fulfill the mitzvah when we make car payments or pay club membership dues, highway tolls and perhaps even taxes that pay for municipal services. When we are posting these payments, we should remember the mitzvah to ensure receiving the appropriate reward.

We Can Do Even Better

With some bills, especially with those for which we won't incur late fees, we take our time. Examples include tuition payments and babysitters. Some of these bills are hefty, and we may not always have the money exactly when it is due. In such situations, according to the *Chinuch*, we are not violating the mitzvos by not paying on time because we are not willfully withholding payment. However, sometimes we have the money and only delay payment because we consider such a delay the general practice. Or maybe we intend to even the score because in our own business people are late paying us. We might delay payment even when delaying provides no real benefit; that is, the money is not really accruing interest anywhere. In such cases, we have an opportunity to act with greater distinction by paying the bills when they are due simply because it is a mitzvah to do so. For that we will receive untold reward.

Yes and No TOGETHER CAN MAKE SENSE

The Chofetz Chaim writes that whenever one has committed the transgression of delaying the payroll, he has ignored and annulled the positive mitzvah of paying on time. This suggests that the two mitzvos, the one positive and the other negative, require the exact same behavior. One might ask why both mitzvos are necessary.

Quite a few mitzvah pairs present one positive mitzvah and one negative mitzvah that require the same behavior. Of the seventy-seven affirmative instructions that the Chofetz Chaim lists as operative today, nineteen of them have corresponding prohibitions. That is a significant percentage of the total. Why are these nineteen singled out for repetition?

Earlier, I suggested that positive mitzvos are stated as positives because they are beneficial to us, while mitzvos stated as prohibitions protect us from harming ourselves. To extend the concept, perhaps a positive mitzvah coexisting with a negative mitzvah could either benefit us or harm us, but not produce neutral results.

I have not analyzed each instance of coexisting positive and negative mitzvos to determine if this rule is generally true. However, we might apply the rule to the three pairs presented here: "Relieve everyone" and "Don't pass up an opportunity," "Give charity" and "Don't be a tightwad," and "Make the payroll on time" and "Don't delay." To demonstrate, I will make the last pair—"Make the payroll on time" and "Don't delay"—my prototype.

Someone who pays his workers on time can easily anticipate the benefits: He will certainly earn his employees' loyalty (as long as other negative factors don't cancel out this positive one) and ensure that his employees are able to focus on their work without worrying about when they will get their paychecks. On the other hand, if an employer delays payment to his employees, he can anticipate harmful effects: His business will likely suffer from poor morale and may even experience a shortage of qualified personnel because the disgruntled employees will find new jobs.

As appropriate as the above explanations seem, they are probably not true. The purpose of the Torah is not to teach good business strategy. Moreover, certain details of these mitzvos do not constitute good business advice. For example, the employer has not violated the mitzvos unless he has the money when payment is due and withholds it; if he does not have the money, the mitzvos do not apply. Employees will feel dissatisfied whether their employer is intentionally withholding the money or whether he simply doesn't have it, so had good business advice been the Torah's primary goal, the mitzvos would have been more stringent. The mitzvos also don't apply if the payroll is not due until some time after the mitzvos demand. For example, for a pay period ending at noon on Monday, the mitzvos instruct that the employer pays by Monday evening, but if the employee agrees to let his employer pay him on Tuesday for the period ending the preceding day, that agreement overrides the mitzvos. Obviously, though, if the employer is late with the Tuesday payment, the employee will react to receiving late payment, just as he would if the mitzvos had applied.

Instead of looking for financial benefits or penalties that one might accrue if he adheres to the mitzvos, he should look for something more personal, something inside of him, something that defines who and what he is—his attitudes and his worldview.

Consider an employer who has the money but nevertheless fails to pay his workers on time. He is demonstrating and reinforcing a fear of parting with money, a fear that he will not be able to replace the money; a fear that his well-being is at risk and that the Almighty is not helping. Reinforcing any one of these fears is harmfully self-defeating because such reinforcement suggests that he believes that his abilities will falter, his health will fail or some unkind force will overcome him at any moment and he will not be able to replace the funds.

On the other hand, if he rushes to ensure that he pays his employees in a timely fashion (that is, in accordance with the mitzvah), then he is partnering with the Almighty. He is demonstrating recognition that the Almighty has selected him to deliver the sustenance that He has decreed to this employee. One immeasurable and unassailable benefit of complying with the mitzvah is the self-esteem the employer will build as he acknowledges that he has been singled out for this Divine task.

PUT IT INTO ACTION!

Have in mind the mitzvah of "Make the Payroll on Time, Don't Delay" when:

- You pay your bills in a timely fashion.
- You pay promptly for any service (e.g., tutoring, babysitting, cleaning, shoe repair, taxi/bus, etc.).
- You calculate the payroll and/or sign the paychecks for your employees.

Notes and Observations

כִּי תָבֹא בְּכֶרֶם רֵעֶךָ וְאָכַלְתָּ עֲנָבִים
כִּי תָבֹא בְּקָמַת רֵעֶךָ וְקָטַפְתָּ מְלִילֹת

**"When you come into your fellow's vineyard,
then you may eat ....
When you come into your fellow's standing grain,
you may pluck the ears" (Deut. 23:25-26)**

Indulge the Employees

The Basic Instruction

In a series of verses, the Torah states, "When you come into your fellow's vineyard, then you may eat .... When you come into your fellow's standing grain, you may pluck the ears" (Deut. 23:25-26). The Sages explain that these verses refer to farm workers (as opposed to someone who just happens to enter a field), and that they instruct a farm owner to allow his laborers to eat from that farm's produce. The Chofetz Chaim lists this mitzvah as number 65 in his list of positives, and the *Chinuch* discusses it under mitzvah number 576.

Let's Discuss

This rule only applies when the work that the laborer does completes the process by which the food becomes liable to a tithe. (Tithes refer to the mitzvos that instruct farmers in Israel to give away certain portions of their harvest, but the details of these tithe mitzvos are not directly relevant here.) On the other hand, the rule even applies to farm labor outside of Israel, where farmers are not required to take tithes. I only mention tithes to define the type of labor covered by the mitzvah to allow laborers to eat. The obligation to take tithes arises at different points in the harvesting cycle, depending on the nature of the produce that the laborers are harvesting. Thus, the mitzvah entitles a laborer to eat only while the laborer is performing the particular task that makes the produce ready for tithing. (For the purpose of this mitzvah, challah is a form of tithe; it is a portion that one must take from bread dough and give to a kohen. The Chofetz Chaim says that someone working on making bread dough should be allowed to eat from the dough.)

In Spirit, We Do This All the Time!

Most of us are urban dwellers and do not have occasion to practice this mitzvah in its literal form. However, we can surely receive reward for exercising the spirit of the mitzvah. The *Chinuch* offers us a way of understanding the spirit of the mitzvah.

The *Chinuch* says that, at its root, the mitzvah encourages us to develop a refined character and show good will to all. He elaborates by describing how joyful it is to finally reap the harvest. Reaping the harvest is the culmination of much hard work that the Almighty has blessed with success. The *Chinuch* says that the Torah desires us to include those who work for us in the festivity of a good harvest; we should not mean-spiritedly treat them as outsiders. The *Chinuch* concludes his discussion of this mitzvah by declaring that the rule is "measure for measure," so good things will follow people who practice good will while bad things will pursue those of evil temperament.

What is "good will"? In reference to the harvesting mitzvah, good will is helping people satisfy normal, harmless temptations, rather than barring people from indulging them. When someone is working in food preparation, especially in its final stages, it is only natural that he would develop an appetite for the food, as well as a desire to ensure that it is, indeed, of good quality. Perhaps, with this mitzvah, the Torah is accommodating a natural desire that would be too tempting to resist.

We have many opportunities to similarly accommodate the natural desires of others. Anyone who employs a maid probably seeks her assistance in food preparation from time to time. On these occasions, the employer assumes that the maid will taste the food. In order to ensure reward miles to Heaven, the employer should keep the mitzvah in mind while she allows her maid to taste the food.

Making a simcha is another opportunity to participate in the spirit of the mitzvah. When we make a simcha, the contract with the caterer often requires us to feed the waiters and the members of the band. Sometimes, we may resent this requirement and unexpected expense. Usually, we only comply because we have to. We might consider complying with a better feeling and a more distinguished bearing by realizing that the extra mouths belong to people who are working on the final preparation of the food: The waiters are serving the food in an elegant manner, and the band is providing the atmosphere that turns the meal into a lavish banquet. In this sense, the workers are truly putting the final touches on the meal, and the spirit of the mitzvah suggests that they deserve a share in the food. My friend Russ Myers, a band leader, shared with me how demeaning it is when the host begrudges the waiters and musicians a meal.

Any employer in the business of preparing food for sale can engage in the spirit of this mitzvah by allowing his employees to indulge their natural appetites. He can do this without disrupting the efficiencies necessary for modern food production. For example, a famous chocolate manufacturer, where my good friend's mother used to work, has an interesting policy: All employees can purchase unlimited product at significant discounts. The discounts allow them to satisfy their natural desires to taste the delicious product without having to sneak chocolate off the production line.

Another friend, Alan Kleiman, told me about an incident that exemplifies how the spirit of the mitzvah can improve business profits: A business that manufactured a complete line of high-quality bathroom accessories was experiencing significant inventory shrinkage. Management suspected that employees were pilfering goods in large quantities. The easiest place from which to steal was the warehouse where the goods were stored for shipping in boxes of twenty-four. That meant that employees were stealing twenty-four goods at a time, more than anyone probably wanted. Rather than incur the expense of additional security, management decided to install a display case containing samples of every item manufactured, and informed the employees that they were free to take whatever they wanted. Once the employees were allowed to take the one or two samples (instead of twenty-four) that they desired for personal use, management reported that inventory shrinkage decreased by two thirds. The result was an annual saving of $200,000! In other words, complying with the spirit of the Torah's instruction resulted in a profit.

The COATTAILS *of the* MITZVAH

We must be careful when describing what we think is the spirit of a mitzvah. Divine laws, unlike man-made laws, may not have a "spirit" that we can comprehend.

Men make laws in order to define acceptable behavior. However, they often don't write the laws clearly enough, and (either intentionally or unintentionally) people can and do misinterpret the laws, or find "loopholes." The lawmaker's original intention is called the "spirit of the law."

The Almighty also wrote laws to describe acceptable behavior, but since He can do anything, He wrote the laws perfectly. Had G-d wanted a broader law or a narrower one, He would have written the laws differently. The Torah leaves no loopholes.

If no loopholes exist in Torah, then can anything exist beyond the letter of the law? According to the *Chinuch*'s comments above, yes, but to distinguish the spirit of G-d's laws from the spirit of man-made laws, one might consider using a different term; instead of saying "the spirit of the law," one might say something like, "the coattails of the mitzvah."

Maimonides first mentions the well-known principle of going "*lifnim mishuras hadin*" (beyond the line of the law) in his explanation of the mitzvah to be like G-d. He says that Jews must exhibit mid-type behavior (i.e., behavior that is midway between stingy and profligate, or midway between lazy and hyperactive). However, the giant Sages of yesteryear always leaned a little toward one extreme, thus going beyond the midpoint, beyond the line of the law.

In his examples, Maimonides does not describe which way to lean. One might surmise from this omission that the correct leaning is not easily discernible, and would vary according to the situation. To decide which way to go beyond the line of the law, one must consult closely with the words of the Sages, whose purpose was to teach the laws.

The *Chinuch* is important as a source text for many reasons, one of which is that he so often describes which behavior one should carry in on the coattails of the mitzvah. For example, about the mitzvah of indulging one's employees, the *Chinuch* says that the Torah is instructing employers to manifest good will toward all workers.

PUT IT INTO ACTION!

Have in mind the mitzvah of "Indulge the Employees" when:

- Working in a group, you share the credit for a noticeable achievement.
- If you manage kitchen help (professionally or at home), you let them taste the food they are preparing.
- Arranging for a party (e.g., wedding, bar mitzvah), you include an allowance for the servers to eat.

Notes and Observations

לֹא תָנִיף עַל קָמַת רֵעֶךָ

"But you shall not lift a sickle to your fellow's standing grain" (Deut. 23:26)

Don't Take Early Lunch Breaks

While the employer must allow the farm laborers to eat, the laborers must comply with two prohibitions against taking advantage of the employer. These prohibitive mitzvos give a worker more frequent opportunities to earn reward miles while he behaves in his normal manner. All he needs to add to his normal behavior is the conscious awareness that he is fulfilling this mitzvah.

The Basic Instruction

A laborer must not take produce at times when taking it interferes with the work, or when taking it would hinder the process that readies the produce for tithing. This instruction appears in the verse, "but you shall not lift a sickle to your fellow's standing grain" (Deut. 23:26). The Chofetz Chaim presents it as number 186 in his list of negatives, and the *Chinuch* discusses it under mitzvah number 577.

Let's Discuss

In deference to this mitzvah, the Sages decreed a limitation on the mitzvah that instructs an employer to indulge his employees:

According to the Rabbis, a worker should only eat of the farm's produce when he is walking from one task to another, because idling during paid hours constitutes theft from the employer. Although other commandments against theft exist, the Almighty recognized the propensity to steal by idling at work, and gave a special mitzvah to forbid workers from indulging that propensity.

We Often Avoid This

I call this mitzvah, "Don't take early lunch breaks," because it is by complying with break etiquette that workers most commonly fulfill the mitzvah. Workers are often careful to wait for an appropriate break time before leaving, and they hurry back after the break to avoid getting a bad reputation at work. If they remembered that not idling at work is a mitzvah, they would garner an extra reward for the self-discipline they are exercising anyway. Even if one is already being fastidious about his work ethic because of the "do not steal" and "do not rob" mitzvos, he can earn extra reward by also keeping this mitzvah in mind.

PUT IT INTO ACTION!

Have in mind the mitzvah of "Don't Take Early Lunch Breaks" when:

- You rush to make it to work on time.
- You make sure to return on time from lunch or a coffee break.

Notes and Observations

וְאֶל־כֶּלְיְךָ לֹא תִתֵּן

"But you shall not put any into your vessel"
(Deut. 23:25)

Don't Pad the Expense Account

The Basic Instruction

Even when a worker is allowed to take food, he may not take an excessive amount. This instruction comes from the verse, "but you shall not put any into your vessel" (Deut. 23:25). The Chofetz Chaim presents it as number 187 in his list of negatives, and the *Chinuch* discusses it under mitzvah number 578.

Let's Discuss

Excessive taking includes taking food for later or taking food for others, even for one's family. The only amount the worker may take is the amount that he wishes to eat while working. Again, the prohibition against excessive taking is already covered by the prohibitions against stealing and robbing, but the Torah provides an extra mitzvah for excessive taking because it is particularly tempting. A similar temptation is "padding the expense account."

We Often Avoid This

Many employees spend personal money on behalf of their employers, and then seek reimbursement via an employee expense report. Again, the worker is entitled to a certain amount (i.e., to cover a reasonable meal during a business lunch), but he may not seek reimbursement for personal expenses. The temptation to slip in a personal expense may be strong, but workers often resist it out of fear of being caught and being embarrassed. Embarrassment is a powerful control mechanism, and it is normal and reasonable that we would act in certain ways to avoid it. However, if we are also conscious of the mitzvos as we control our desires, we will earn additional reward. Awareness of this mitzvah will also strengthen our resolve to resist temptation.

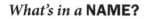

What's in a NAME?

Some readers might take issue with my modern-sounding names for many of the mitzvos, such as "Don't take early lunch breaks" and "Don't pad the expense account." Admittedly, my suggested names are transparent and light-hearted attempts at engaging the reader's attention. In defense of the liberties I have taken with the real names of the mitzvos, mitzvos do not seem to have "real names." Each source book seems to choose its own mitzvah names. For example, in *Mishneh Torah*, Maimonides calls the "Don't take early lunch breaks" mitzvah, "A laborer may not eat from the standing crop during work." The *Chinuch* shortened Maimonides' title to "A laborer may not eat during work," but the Chofetz Chaim lengthened it to, "A laborer may not eat while working on produce that grows from the ground except at the end of work."

In some sources, the words of the verse become the title of the mitzvah. This titling strategy works best when the verse is short and to the point (i.e., "Don't murder," "Don't steal" or "Honor your father and mother"). However, a verse often requires an explanation from the Oral Torah, in which case the verse doesn't work as a title. For example, the prohibition against eating on the job comes from a verse that states, "You shall not lift a sickle to your fellow's standing grain." The words of the verse alone don't tell the reader that the mitzvah refers to a hired hand while he is working. The written verse needs its oral counterpart. Therefore, Maimonides, quite reasonably, felt it was justified, and perhaps even necessary, to invent concise titles for the mitzvos. What remains puzzling is why the *Chinuch*, who followed Maimonides, and especially the Chofetz Chaim, who followed both, decided to invent their own titles. Whatever their reasons, their precedent emboldened me to invent titles that suggest the modern-day activities that the mitzvos cover.

PUT IT INTO ACTION!

Have in mind the mitzvah of "Don't Pad the Expense Account" when:

- You fill out an expense claim carefully and honestly.

Notes and Observations

וְעָשִׂיתָ מַעֲקֶה לְגַגֶּךָ
וְלֹא־תָשִׂים דָּמִים בְּבֵיתֶךָ

"You shall make a parapet for your roof and not bring blood upon your house" (Deut. 22:8)

Fence Off Danger; Don't Ignore It

The Basic Instruction

The Torah states, "When you build a new house then you shall make a parapet for your roof and not bring blood upon your house if anyone were to fall from there" (Deut. 22: 8). From this verse come two mitzvos, one positive and the other negative, which, according to the *Chinuch*, mirror each other. They instruct us to prevent danger on our property by installing the necessary safety measures. The Chofetz Chaim presents these mitzvos as the 75th in his list of positives and the 190th in his list of negatives. The *Chinuch* numbers these mitzvos 546 and 547.

Let's Discuss

Perhaps, the most practical reason for these mitzvos is the guidelines they provide for risk-taking. We all take precautions to minimize risk, but we frequently agonize over the appropriate balance between cost and benefit. For example, who knows for sure how much to spend on a burglar alarm system, which level of life insurance to buy, or the amount of time one can afford to take his eyes off his toddler?

The *Chinuch* helps by presenting some examples of what he

considers dangerous: A high place is dangerous if it does not have a fence of ten *tefachim*. (This measurement equals about forty inches and, interestingly, is close to the fence height required by most modern building codes.) A fence of ten *tefachim* is high enough to prevent a child (but not an adult) from climbing over, and high enough to keep an adult from falling by accident. These specifications suggest that we are responsible for minimizing the danger, but we are not obligated to eliminate it completely.

To minimize the risk of ingesting poison, the *Chinuch* explains that one is not allowed to drink water if its container was left uncovered long enough for a poisonous animal or insect to have approached it, drunk from it and left (the fear being that the animal's saliva poisoned the water). This prohibition only applies in regions infested with poisonous snakes or insects. In other words, for the prohibition to apply, the risk must be real. However, one need not have observed a poisonous animal in the vicinity for the risk to be considered real; if the *possibility* exists, the water is dangerous. This instruction sends the message that we must protect ourselves even from relatively low risk.

In today's statistically oriented society, the absence of a numeric quantification for danger might be frustrating. Must we install safeguards when the probability of risk is five percent? Ten percent? Forty percent? The truth is, when faced with real-life dangers, we seldom have firm probability readings. Perhaps that is why the *Chinuch* provided the real-life examples that he did; their range and context help us to determine the necessary degrees of precaution to exercise in our own situations.

We Do This All the Time!

We install railings around our porches and decks, and then inspect them periodically to make sure that they are still sturdy. We clean our rain gutters to prevent heavy icicles from forming. We service the furnace to ensure that it functions efficiently and safely. We install smoke alarms and carbon monoxide detectors to provide early warnings of danger. We service the car regularly to ensure safe steering and braking. We childproof the house in a hundred different ways and constantly come up with even more ways.

Risk-proofing our homes takes up a good deal of our spare time. We should relish, rather than resent these chores, because through them we perform this positive mitzvah and avoid the prohibition. By keeping these two mitzvos in mind, we can align ourselves with the will of the Almighty and perform frequent holy acts. Such awareness will reward us with both immeasurable peace in the World To Come and the peace of mind that we seek in this world.

We can reap even deeper benefits from "fencing off danger" by considering the *Chinuch*'s thoughts on reconciling the implications of these mitzvos with the axiom that the Almighty controls every occurrence, good or bad, according to a person's merit or guilt. According to the *Talmud Bavli, Hullin* 7b, "A man does not hurt his finger below (on earth) unless it is proclaimed for him above (in heaven)." If that is so, then why bother risk-proofing our homes? Wouldn't we be making better use of our time by simply working to accrue merit in the eyes of the Almighty?

The *Chinuch* explains that the Almighty willed us to live in a world of predictable events that we call the laws of nature. For example, we can predict that fire will burn and that water will extinguish. The Almighty further willed us to be subject to those laws, and blessed us with the common sense to govern ourselves safely in accordance with them. If someone ignores the Almighty's natural laws, he is violating the Almighty's will and inviting retribution. For example, if a person who is ordinarily righteous, honorable and deserving of the highest accolades ignores the Almighty's immutable law of gravity and throws himself off a cliff, his defiance of the Almighty's will alone warrants a death penalty.

However, it is the Almighty, not the natural law, Who controls a person's fate down to the smallest detail. One might best describe the natural law as the Almighty's typical decisions. Sometimes He makes an atypical decision, thereby defying the natural law. We call His atypical decisions "miracles" (when we recognize them).

The people who most often recognize miracles are those who have trained themselves in the Almighty's reality, people who regularly see through the veil of the laws of nature to glimpse, instead, the laws of the Almighty. As an example of such a person, the *Chinuch* cites our forefather Abraham. When the tyrant Nimrod threatened to throw Abraham into a fiery furnace if he refused to bow to idols, Abraham chose the furnace. His defiance was a principled act, but not a highly unusual one; many people have sacrificed their lives for an ideal. As the *Chinuch* explains, Abraham became a stellar model of devotion not because of his willingness to sacrifice, but because of his intense clarity: He understood that G-d's desire for him to refuse to bow to idols was at least as strong, if not stronger, than G-d's normal desire for fire to burn. Abraham was not challenging or ignoring the natural law; he was just intensely aware of a superior law. Consequently, when the fire did not burn him, Abraham was not surprised. (Nimrod, on the other hand, as well as the others who witnessed the incident, considered what they had seen to be a miracle and let Abraham be.)

A pithier example comes from an exchange that the Steipler Rav had with a skeptic: The skeptic scoffed at the Midrash that predicts that, in the time of Moshiach, bread will grow on trees. "How can bread possibly grow on trees?" said the skeptic. Ignoring the opportunity to explain, the Steipler Rav skipped to the heart of the matter and replied, "And bananas you understand?"

By increasing our awareness of the "fence off danger" mitzvah, we can gain a sublime wisdom about the events and conditions of the risks we encounter, and feel confident of our place in the greater scheme of things.

PUT IT INTO ACTION!

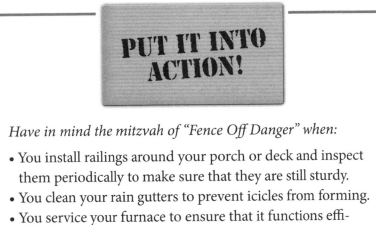

Have in mind the mitzvah of "Fence Off Danger" when:

- You install railings around your porch or deck and inspect them periodically to make sure that they are still sturdy.
- You clean your rain gutters to prevent icicles from forming.
- You service your furnace to ensure that it functions efficiently and safely.
- You install smoke alarms and carbon monoxide detectors to provide early warnings of danger.
- You service your car regularly to ensure it's safe.
- You childproof your house.

Notes and Observations

וְכִי־תִמְכְּרוּ מִמְכָּר לַעֲמִיתֶךָ אוֹ קָנֹה מִיַּד עֲמִיתֶךָ

"When you sell something to your fellow or buy from your fellow's hand ..." (Lev. 25:14)

Let's Make a Deal

The Basic Instruction

The Torah states, "When you sell something to your fellow or buy from your fellow's hand ..." (Lev. 25:14). This verse is instructing Jewish courts to settle business disputes in accordance with the commercial concepts and rules from the Oral Torah. The Chofetz Chaim presents this mitzvah as number 67 in his list of positives, and the *Chinuch* discusses it under mitzvah number 336.

Let's Discuss

When a dispute arises, a Jewish court first attempts arbitration to find a solution that is acceptable to both parties. Many disputes concern commercial activity. My daughter is currently involved in such a dispute. Her store sells costume jewelry. She agreed to try to sell the products of a certain craftsman from her community. Once the goods arrived at her store, the craftsman requested payment. However, the goods were on consignment, which meant that my daughter wasn't obligated to pay until the goods sold. When she wouldn't pay, the craftsman insisted that the goods were not, in fact, meant for consignment but for final sale. He maintained that payment was due. Since neither party has paperwork to prove anything, and since the goods still haven't sold, the disagreement persists. Often, disputes arise over the proper interpretation of a contract. If the contract includes a set of rules that differ from those identified by the Torah, the Jewish court must judge according to the details of the contract. On any issue about which the contract is silent, the court must consult the Torah rules.

Many Torah rules address commercial activity, and the *Chinuch* lists quite a few of them, referring the reader to the source literature that deals with the rules in the detail they demand. One issue that the *Chinuch* emphasizes is that the Torah requires a *kinyan*, a formal act of acquisition, to complete a sale. Even though the Chofetz Chaim writes more briefly, he also mentions the concept of a *kinyan*, underscoring its importance.

Various actions can formally constitute a *kinyan*. For land, a *kinyan* can consist of a deed transfer, a demonstration of ownership or the payment of money. However, for movable goods, paying money does not qualify as a valid *kinyan*. Rather, one must acquire movable goods by demonstrating ownership. That is, one must lift the object, move it or take hold of its controls (such as the reins of an animal or the key of a car). In all cases, a *kinyan* that the buyer executes is only valid if the seller is a willing participant. Without a *kinyan*, no transaction legally took place and no legal requirement to "keep one's word" exists. That is, statements of intent are not binding, no matter how sincere or how strongly demonstrated. Even paying a deposit isn't enough, because without a *kinyan* either party can refund the deposit and back out. However, out of distaste for someone who reneges on his word, the Sages composed a curse that a court could declare against such a person:

"He who exacted payment from the people of the generation of the Flood, from the people of the generation of the Dispersal, from the people of Sodom and Gomorrah and from Egypt who drowned in the sea, He will exact payment from one who does not stand by his word."

Such a curse certainly encourages people to keep their word, yet still allows trustworthiness to be an expression of character, rather than just an act of obedience to the law.

We Do This All the Time!

This mitzvah obliges us to clarify the details of our business dealings, and to stand by our word. We do this all the time and should keep the mitzvah in mind. Although one could argue that, strictly speaking, clarifying a business deal or transaction is not performing the actual mitzvah (since the mitzvah technically pertains only to the judges of a Jewish court), it still qualifies as the coattails of the mitzvah. We can earn reward for that.

Every time we shop at a store that is not self-serve, say "I'll take that" and then complete the transaction, we are participating in the buying-and-selling mitzvah by keeping our word. We should stay conscious of the mitzvah, especially if the proprietor who is anxious to complete the sale is the one serving us. (An employee may not care one way or the other.)

For more serious transactions, such as major purchases, employment agreements or business partnerships, one party might write up a contract that the other party has to carefully review, and for which that other party will perhaps request revisions. Fine-tuning such a contract also constitutes participating in a mitzvah: Preventing disputes ensures that both parties will adhere to the contract. Reviewing a contract is often a tedious process that one or both parties would sooner forgo. We usually hope that every business deal will proceed smoothly, exactly as anticipated. When one doesn't, the ramifications, which come directly from the contract, can be a rude awakening. Remembering the mitzvah can soften the blow. With mitzvah consciousness, we will be more patient and have more interest in the process of fine-tuning the contract details. Consequently, we will enjoy that immediate benefit of added protection, in addition to the mitzvah reward.

We Can Do Even Better

Many retail stores have a full-refund policy. Some advertise a "no questions asked" policy (although they often ask anyway). The question that arises for us is whether or not returns are acceptable. On the one hand, these stores have set the rules of business by sanctioning refunds. On the other hand, the Sages directed their "He who exacted payment" curse at people who take advantage of non-binding sales (sales that lacked a *kinyan*), so perhaps the curse applies equally to people who take advantage of today's non-binding sales (sales that allow refunds).

I started thinking about this when Eatons, a major department store in Canada, went bankrupt. They had been in operation for three generations. Their claim to fame had been their groundbreaking, full-refund, "no questions asked" guarantee. Their demise made headlines across the nation.

Many people wrote to the newspapers relating stories of how, in their youth, they had regularly purchased items from Eatons, used the items for the appropriate season and then returned them for a full refund. Some expressed pride for their conniving cleverness and chutzpah, while others expressed sadness at having contributed to the downfall of their favorite store. One memorable story came from a woman who said that her teenage brother bought a new lawnmower at the beginning of each summer. He would use the lawnmower all summer, earning money by mowing other people's lawns. At the end of the season, he would return the lawnmower, claiming that he wasn't happy with the way it worked. He always received a full refund for something that he had used profitably. Was this what the store had had in mind when they instituted their full-refund policy?

Certainly, we should not feel constrained from returning defective merchandise, or merchandise that didn't fit the child we hoped it would fit, didn't match the drapes we hoped it would match, etc. Stores make refund policies to increase their sales; the security of the refund policy probably makes shoppers more willing to buy things that they wouldn't otherwise buy. However, small, independent retailers may only post the full-refund policy because they have to follow the lead of the major retailers. Further, no retailer, big or small, benefits from taking back merchandise like the lawnmower that has already served its purpose; or from unused merchandise whose selling season has passed because we neglected to return it promptly. If we find ourselves in such a situation, we should consult a Rav.

PUT IT INTO ACTION!

Have in mind the mitzvah of "Let's Make a Deal" when:

- You negotiate a contract with a supplier or customer.
- You review all the details of a major purchase (e.g., a car or a computer system), such as the terms, warranty and the like.
- You complete a transaction for any purchase.

Notes and Observations

Speaking of Refunds, This Sale is Final

After discussing store refunds, I want to reiterate G-d's refund policy: When, after one hundred and twenty years, we "come back" to the Heavenly register with the mitzvah items that we have "bought" from His store, G-d will provide a refund so full that it is actually, according to the Sages, a reward. It is a refund of the spiritual energy that we spent on Earth. (Remember how tiring a mitzvah can be? One could interpret that tiredness as the result of spending spiritual energy. The same could apply if the mitzvah is expensive, unexpected, confusing or inconvenient.) Maybe we will find that when the spiritual energy we spent on Earth is refunded in whatever currency form it takes in Heaven, it buys a lot more. Maybe that's why the Sages described this phenomenal exchange rate as a reward.

Whether or not you find this analogy a useful insight, please understand and appreciate the following: First, the results that await us in Heaven are a direct consequence of our efforts here on Earth. Second, the body is too limited to be the main recipient of the vastness envisioned for Heaven; the primary recipient must be the soul. The conclusion we must reach then is that the more we exercise and expand our mind and soul—by maintaining conscious awareness of each mitzvah that we perform—the more capacity we will have to enjoy the vast rewards promised us in Heaven. *Keep it in mind!*

APPENDICES

APPENDIX I
Translation of the sources for *"Mitzvos Tzrichos Kavana"* —mitzvos require intent

APPENDIX II
Helpful Ideas for Putting This Book into Practice

APPENDIX III
The Mitzvah Misdeed

APPENDIX I

Translation of the Sources for "*Mitzvos Tzrichos Kavana*" —Mitzvos Require Intent

I encourage the reader to review the original Hebrew text of the *Shulchan Aruch* and *Mishnah Berurah*, and have extracted it below to facilitate this. Since I often find that I gain new insights into the material whenever I am able to consult an English translation after reading the original Hebrew, I have also provided an English translation of these Hebrew texts, with some explanatory notes of my own.

Shulchan Aruch, Orech Chaim 60:4

ד (ז) *יש אומרים שאין מצוות צריכות כוונה
*ויש אומרים (ח) שצריכות כוונה (ט) *לצאת
בעשיית אותה מצוה (י) *וכן הלכה:

Some say[7] that mitzvos do not require conscious intent when performed, while others say they do require intent[8] in order to fulfill[9] the performance of that mitzvah and such is the law[10].

Mishnah Berurah

(ז) יש אומרים. דע דלפי המתבאר מן הפוסקים שני כונות יש למצוה א׳ כונת הלב למצוה עצמה וב׳ כונה לצאת בה דהיינו שיכוין לקיים בזה כאשר צוה ד׳ כמו שכתב הב״ח בסי׳ ח׳ וכונת המצוה שנזכר בזה הסעיף אין תלוי כלל בכונת

[7]**Some say.** According to the legal experts, one must have two intentions while performing a mitzvah: One is the intent of the heart regarding the mitzvah

itself, and the second is the intent to fulfill the mitzvah, meaning, to fulfill with this action what G-d commanded [us to do], as the Bach writes in chapter 8*. The "intent" of the mitzvah mentioned in this paragraph does not depend at all on the first type of intent, the intent of the heart regarding the mitzvah itself, which involves directing his heart to that which he is expressing with his mouth and not thinking in his heart of other matters. Examples of that kind of intent—of things that people should say without distraction—are the *Shema*, the prayers (i.e., the *Amidah*), Grace after meals and the *Kiddush*. Everyone agrees that ideally the mitzvah requires this conscious intent of the heart, but, after the fact, if someone did not consciously direct his heart, he has nevertheless fulfilled the mitzvah, providing he maintained awareness at least during the first verse of the *Shema* (when reciting the *Shema*) and the blessing of "*Avos*" (the first blessing) in prayer (the *Amidah*), as explained later.

הלב למצוה עצמה שיכוין בלבו למה שהוא מוציא מפיו ואל יהרהר בלבו לד"א כגון בק"ש ותפילה ובהמ"ז וקידוש וכדומה דזה לכו"ע לכתחילה מצוה שיכוין בלבו ובדיעבד אם לא כיון יצא לבד מפסוק ראשון של ק"ש וברכת אבות של תפילה כמו שמבואר לקמן רק שמחולקים בענין אם חייב לכוין קודם שמתחיל המצוה לצאת בעשיית אותה המצוה. ולמצוה מן המובחר כו"ע מודים דצריך כונה כדאיתא בנדרים ראב"צ אומר עשה דברים לשם פועלם ונאמר ותהי יראתם אותי מצות אנשים מלומדה וכמו שכתב הגר"א על הא דאיתא בסימן ח' עי"ש:

* In *Orech Chaim*, Chapter 8, the *Tur* writes regarding tzitzis: "While wrapping oneself in the tallis, one should have in mind that the Almighty commanded us to wrap ourselves with the tallis so that we should remember all the commandments, to perform them." On this the Bach comments: "The *Tur* is teaching that the main upholding of the commandment depends upon the intent one maintains at the time of upholding the commandment. This is not true of the other commandments, where one fulfills his obligation even when he intended nothing other than that he was performing the commandments in the Name of G-d who commanded him to perform them."

Rather, in this paragraph the legal experts are disputing the issue of whether one is obligated to consciously intend before beginning the mitzvah to discharge his duty with the performance of that mitzvah. Furthermore, (in this as well) everyone agrees that to perform the mitzvah in the best possible way, one must have such intent, as it says in *Maseches Nedarim* (62a): "Rabbi Eliezer ben Tzadok says: Do good deeds for the sake of their Maker," and it is said (Isaiah 29:13), "… and their fear of Me is but the routine precept of people," and as the *Gra* writes on that which is found in chapter 8, see there (par. 8).

(ח) שצריכות כונה. ואם לא כיון לצאת ידי חובתו בעשיית המצוה לא יצא מן התורה וצריך לחזור ולעשותה. ואפילו אם ספק לו אם כיון אם הוא מצוה דאורייתא ספיקא לחומרא כ"כ הפמ"ג בסימן תקפ"ט עי"ש. ונ"ל דלא יברך אז על המצוה דבלא"ה יש כמה דיעות בענין הברכה אפילו אם ודאי לא כיון בראשונה:

[8]**They do require intent.** And if he did not maintain awareness to discharge his obligation through the performance of the mitzvah, he has not fulfilled his Torah duty and must return and perform it again. Even if it is only a doubt whether he acted consciously, he must perform it again if it is a Biblical command, for which uncertainties are presumed unfulfilled. Thus writes the *Pri Megadim* in Chapter 589; examine there. However, it seems to me that in such a case he should not recite the blessing upon the second performance of the mitzvah, because even without this condition of doubt, there are numerous opinions regarding the blessing (whether it should be recited a second time), even in a case where he knows for certain that he did not act with intent the first time.

(ט) לצאת. לפיכך התוקע להתלמד או המברך בהמ"ז עם קטנים לחנכם במצות והוא היה ג"כ חייב בבהמ"ז ושכח אז להתכוין לצאת בה ג"כ עבור עצמו וכן

[9]**To fulfill.** Therefore, someone blowing a shofar to practice, or someone pronouncing the

כה״ג בכל המצות שעשאם לשום איזה ענין לא יצא ידי חובתו ועיין בט״ז בסימן תפ״ט שמוכח מדבריו דהמברך עם קטנים הנ״ל לא יצא אפילו למ״ד מצות אין צריכות כוונה דהוי כמכוין בפירוש שלא לצאת ואם כונתו בעשיית המצוה לשום איזה ענין וגם לצאת בה ידי המצוה יצא:

Grace after meals with youngsters to educate them in the mitzvos when he himself was obligated to say Grace, and he forgot to intend to fulfill his own obligation with that reading, and similarly for any mitzvah that he performed with any other focus, he has not fulfilled his obligation. See *Taz*, Chapter 489 [par. 4], from whose words it appears clear that one who pronounces a blessing with youngsters in the manner described above has not fulfilled his obligation even according to the authority that says that mitzvos do not require intention, because in this situation it is considered as if he intended expressly not to fulfill his obligation. However, if his intention while performing the mitzvah was with some other focus and also to fulfill the mitzvah, then he has fulfilled it.

(י) וכן הלכה. כתב המ״א בשם הרדב״ז דזה דוקא במצוה דאורייתא אבל במצוה דרבנן א״צ כונה. ולפ״ז כל הברכות שהם ג״כ דרבנן לבד מבהמ״ז אם לא כיון בהם לצאת יצא בדיעבד אך מכמה מקומות בשו״ע משמע שהוא חולק ע״ז וכן מבאור הגר״א בסימן תפ״ט משמע ג״כ שאין לחלק בין מצוה דאורייתא למצוה דרבנן. ודע דכתב המ״א לקמן בסימן תפ״ט סק״ח דאף דהשו״ע פסק להלכה דמצות צריכות כונה וא״כ היכא שלא כיון בפעם ראשונה צריך לחזור ולעשות המצוה אעפ״כ לא יברך עוד עליה שלענין ברכה צריך לחוש לדעת הי״א שאין צריך כונה ועי׳ בבה״ל. ודע עוד דכתב הח״א בכלל ס״ח דמה דמצרכינן ליה לחזור ולעשות המצוה היינו במקום שיש לתלות שעשייה הראשונה לא היתה לשם מצוה כגון

[10]**And such is the law.** The *Magen Avraham* writes in the name of the *Radvaz* that this is true only with regard to a Biblical mitzvah, but a Rabbinic mitzvah does not require intent. Accordingly, regarding all the blessings—which are all Rabbinic except for Grace after meals—if one did not maintain conscious intent while reciting them to fulfill his obligation, then, after the fact, he is considered to have fulfilled it. However, from various comments it

בתקיעה שהיתה להתלמד או בק״ש שהיתה דרך לימודו וכדומה אבל אם קורא ק״ש כדרך שאנו קורין בסדר תפילה וכן שאכל מצה או תקע ונטל לולב אע״פ שלא כיון לצאת יצא שהרי משום זה עושה כדי לצאת אע״פ שאינו מכוין עכ״ל ור״ל היכא שמוכח לפי הענין שעשייתו הוא כדי לצאת אע״פ שלא כיון בפירוש יצא אבל בסתמא בודאי לא יצא כדאיתא בתוס׳ סוכה [דף ל״ט ע״א ד״ה עובר עי״ש] וכ״ז לענין בדיעבד אבל לכתחילה ודאי צריך ליזהר לכוין קודם כל מצוה לצאת ידי חובת המצוה וכן העתיקו כל האחרונים בספריהם עיין בח״א בכלל כ״א ובדה״ח הלכות ק״ש ובמעשה רב:

seems that the *Shulchan Aruch* differs from this opinion. Similarly, from the comments of the *Gra** on Chapter 489 it also seems that there is no reason to differentiate between a Biblical mitzvah and a Rabbinic one.

Be aware that the *Magen Avraham* writes below in 489:8 that even though the *Shulchan Aruch* concludes that mitzvos require intent, and that therefore where one did not maintain intent the first time he must go back and do the mitzvah again, nevertheless he should not again recite the blessing upon it, because with regard to the blessing one must consider the possible validity of the other opinion, that mitzvos do not require intent. Examine the *Biur Halacha*.

One should also realize that the *Chayei* Adam writes in Section 68 that the requirement to return and perform the mitzvah again applies only when there is cause to conclude

---

*Chapter 489:4 discusses counting the Omer, and the proper manner of responding if someone asks you which day it is to count before you have performed the commandment yourself. In note 7, the *Gra* explains that this issue is only relevant according to the opinion that commandments do not require intent. The *Gra* thus reveals that his own opinion is that there would be no concern of how to respond if commandments must be performed with conscious intent, since in such a situation your intent would only be to answer that person's question, not to fulfill the commandment. However, the *Gra* maintains that the commandment to count the Omer is today a Rabbinic one, and that that's what is being discussed in this chapter. Accordingly, it seems the *Gra* rules that the opinion requiring performance with conscious intent applies to Rabbinic commands, as well.

that the first performance was not done for the purpose of the mitzvah as, for example, when the shofar blowing was for practice, or the Shema was recited in the course of a learning session or something similar. However, if he recited the Shema in the manner that we do during the order of prayers, or if he ate matzah, blew the shofar or held the lulav, then even if he did not consciously intend to fulfill his obligation, he has still fulfilled it, because it is obvious that it was for this reason that he performed the act, in order to fulfill the mitzvah, even though he did not have conscious intent. These are the *Chayei Adam*'s words. What the *Chayei Adam* means is that where it is evident from the situation that his activity was intended to fulfill the mitzvah, even though he did not maintain conscious intent, he has fulfilled it. However, in a neutral situation (i.e., a situation that is not self-evident) he has certainly not fulfilled it, as can be seen from *Tosfos Sukkah* 39a, in the paragraph "*Oveir*."

All of this regards a situation after the fact. But ideally he certainly has to be careful to consciously intend before each mitzvah to fulfill the obligation to do the mitzvah. So all the later authorities have ruled in their books; see *Chayei Adam*, Section 21, the *Derech HaChayim* in the laws of Shema, and the *Maaseh Rav*.

Biur Halacha

Some say that mitzvos do not require conscious intent when performed, whether he does it himself and does not consciously intend to thereby fulfill his obligation, or whether he hears it from another (for example, the Megillah or shofar), and

י״א שאין מצות צ״כ. בין אם הוא עושה בעצמו ואין מתכוין לצאת בה ידי חובה ובין אם שמע מאחר כגון מגילה ושופר ולא התכוין בהשמיעה לצאת בה ידי חובת המצוה (ב״י רי״ג ורי״ט). וה״ה בכל מצות התלויות באמירה כגון ק״ש ובהמ״ז וי״א דבדבר שאין בו אלא אמירה לכו״ע צריכה כונה. ב״י סימן תקפ״ט. וה״מ שמכוין לפעולה זו שהוא עושה רק שאין מכוין לצאת בזה ידי המצוה כגון בענין תקיעות שתוקע לשיר או להתלמד וכדומה בשאר המצות אבל אם הוא מתעסק בעלמא וממילא

עלה המצוה בידו כגון שנופח בשופר ועלה תקיעה בידו וכה"ג בשאר המצות לכו"ע לא יצא. רמב"ן במלחמות בר"ה וש"מ ברכות י"ג ע"א. וכה"ג מוכח מתר"י במ"ש בענין קורא להגיה עי"ש. ודע עוד דדוקא אם הוא יודע שהוא חייב עדיין במצוה זו שהוא עושה אבל אם הוא סבור שהוא פטור ממנה כגון שנטל לולב ביום א' דסוכות וקסבר שהוא ערב סוכות או שקסבר שלולב זה פסול הוא לכו"ע לא יצא. וראיה ממ"ש בסימן תע"ה ס"ד דאם היה סבור שהוא חול או שאין זו מצה לא יצא ידי חובתו והרי במידי דאכילה שאין מתכוין כמתכוין דמי כמ"ש המ"א שם ואעפ"כ לא יצא וא"ל דאעפ"כ יש לדחות דשם הוא לפי מאי דפסקינן בעלמא מצות צריכות כוונה ורק בעניני אכילה מחמת ההנאה שנהנה לא נוכל לבטל עשייתו כאלו לא עשה ונחשב הדבר כאלו מתכוין וע"כ אמרינן דאם לא ידע שהיום פסח לא נוכל לומר עליו כאלו התכוין משא"כ אם נאמר דמצות אין צריכות כוונה בשום פעם גם בכה"ג יצא דז"א דהלא בר"ן בר"ה מביא ראיה לדין זה דאל"ה ל"ל לאבוה דשמואל למינקט כפאוהו פרסיים לאשמעינן יותר רבותא דאפילו בחד מהני גווני יצא וא"כ עדיין תקשי לפי מה דאמר רבא שם ז"א וכו' דקסבר מצות אין צריכות כוונה אלא ודאי דאפילו אין צריכות כונה בכה"ג לא יצא וצע"ג על הרב בעל הלבוש שם דמסיק שם טעם לדין זה דמצות צריכות כוונה. ובמתכוין בפירוש שלא לצאת לכו"ע לא יצא. ב"י בסימן תקפ"ט:

was not focusing while listening to fulfill the mitzvah (*Bais Yosef* 213 and 219). The same would apply for all the mitzvos that depend on speech, such as the Shema and Grace after meals. However, others say that for mitzvos that involve nothing but speech everyone agrees that intent is necessary (*Bais Yosef* 589).

This applies when he intended to perform that particular act but did not intend to fulfill the mitzvah, such as is possible with shofar blasts that he produced for music or to practice, or similar situations with other mitzvos. However, if he was acting without *any* intent and by chance the mitzvah was performed, such as is possible when he blew into the shofar and happened to produce a *tekiah* note or similar situations with other mitzvos, then according to everybody he has not fulfilled the mitzvah. (*Ramban*, commentary on *Maseches Rosh Hashanah*, and *Shita Mekubetzes* on *Berachos* 13a; similar conclusions appear evident from the students of Rabbeinu Yonah, in their comments on "*koreh l'hagiah*"; examine there.)

Know, as well, that he can only fulfill the mitzvah if he realizes that he is actually obligated in this mitzvah that he now performs (unintentionally), but if he thinks that he is exempt from it—as is possible when he took a lulav on the first day of Sukkos thinking it was really the day before, or thinking that the lulav was invalid for the mitzvah—then everyone agrees that he has not fulfilled his obligation. Proof of this can be found from what is written in 475:4, that if someone eating matzah thought that it was a weekday or that it was not matzah he was eating, then he has not fulfilled his obligation. And this is in regard to a mitzvah of eating—where we know that "eating without conscious intent is equivalent to eating with conscious intent," as the *Magen Avraham* writes there—and even so he has not fulfilled his obligation. Nor can one say that this proof could be pushed aside as follows: As a general rule we conclude that mitzvos require intent, and only in the case of eating, which involves pleasure—the presence of which forces us to consider the act valid—is the matter considered as if done intentionally; consequently, we say that if the problem was that he did not know that today was Pesach then we cannot assign to the act conscious intent, but if we conclude as a general rule that mitzvos do not require intent in any instance, then also here he would have fulfilled his obligation.

This argument cannot stand, for does not the *Ra"n* in *Rosh Hashanah* bring a proof to this law, as follows: "For if this were not the case, why did Avuha d'Shmuel need to select the case of 'the Persians forcing him' to demonstrate an extra legal point, for even with only one of these conditions he would fulfill the mitzvah, and if so it would still be problematic according to what Rava said there, 'This is not ...,' since he rules that mitzvos do not require intent."

Therefore, it is certain that even if mitzvos do not require intent, in such circumstances (i.e., ignorance of the obligation) he has not fulfilled the mitzvah. Indeed, it requires a great deal of thought to explain the Rav Baal HaLevush there who concludes there the reason for this ruling is that mitzvos require intent.

In a case where one explicitly intends not to fulfill the mitzvah then all agree he does not fulfill it (*Bais Yosef*, Chapter 589).

וי״א שצריכות כונה. פי׳ מן התורה כן כתב הרשב״ם להדיא בפסחים ד׳ קי״ד ע״ב ד״ה אע״ג וכן משמע פשטי׳ דסוגיא בר״ה ד׳ כ״ח ע״ב בגמרא אבל זכרון תרועה כתיב וכו׳ משמע דפלוגתיהו בדאורייתא וכן כתב הלבוש ושארי אחרונים דלא כהפמ״ג שמסתפק בזה. ודע דכ״ז הוא בשארי המצות אבל מצוה התלוי באכילה כגון כזית מצה בפסח וה״ה אכילת כזית בסוכה בלילה הראשונה דעת השו״ע לקמן בסימן תע״ה ס״ד דיצא בדיעבד אפילו אם לא כיון והב״ח מחמיר שם גם בזה עי״ש. ועיין בב״ח ובפמ״ג בסימן ח׳ ובסימן תרכ״ה דמשמע מדבריהם דמצות ציצית וסוכה הכונה בהם לעיכובא כמו בשאר המצות ולפ״ז אם קראוהו לתורה ולוקח טליתו או טלית הקהל לעלות לבימה שאז זמנו בהול ומסתמא אינו מכוין אז בלבישתו לקיים המ״ע של ציצית ממילא עובר בזה על המ״ע אם לא כשמכוין לשם מצוה ואז יוכל לברך ג״כ והעולם אינם נזהרין בזה ואולי שטעמם דכיון שאין רוצה ללבוש אז את הטלית ואינו לובשו אלא מפני כבוד התורה לשעה קלה אין זה לבישה המחייבתו בציצית דומיא דמי שלובש להראות לקונה מידתו שפטור אז מציצית ועצה היעוצה לעשות כמו שכתב השערי אפרים הבאתי את דבריו לעיל בסימן י״ד ס״ג בבה״ל עי״ש:

And some say they do require intent, meaning that intent is a Torah-mandated obligation. So writes the Rashbam plainly in *Pesachim* 114b, in the paragraph, "*Af al gav*." Similarly, this is implied by the plain meaning of the text in *Rosh Hashanah* 28b, where it says, "but 'remembrance of teruah' is written …," implying that their dispute concerns a Torah-mandated obligation. And so writes the *Levush* and other later authorities, unlike the *Pri Megadim* who maintains a doubt on this issue.

Know further, that all this concerns other mitzvos, but a mitzvah that depends upon eating, such as eating an olive's volume of matzah on Pesach and similarly the consumption of an olive's volume of food in a sukkah on the first night of Sukkos, the opinion of the *Shulchan Aruch* in 475:4 is that after the fact he has fulfilled his obligation even if he did not intend to do the mitzvah. The *Bach*, however, is stringent even in such a case; examine there.

Also examine the *Bach* and *Pri Megadim* in Chapters 8 and 625, where it seems from their words that the mitzvos of tzitzis and sukkah require intent just like the other mitzvos.

According to this, if someone is called up to the Torah and he grabs his tallis or a congregation tallis on his way up to the bimah in a hurry, he probably does not have intent to fulfill the positive mitzvah of tzitzis. He thereby transgresses the positive mitzvah if he does not have intent to fulfill it—and if he does have intent then he can make the blessing, as well. Most people are not careful about this, and perhaps their reason is that, since someone in that situation does not really wish to wear the tallis and is only wearing it out of respect for the Torah for a short time, this is not considered "wearing" that obligates one in the mitzvah of tzitzis. This would be similar to a salesman who dons a garment to show a prospective buyer its size; such a situation would be exempt from the mitzvah of tzitzis. One would be well advised in this situation to follow what the *Shaarei Ephraim* wrote—I have transcribed his words above in 14:3 in the *Biur Halacha*; examine there.

לצאת. עיין במ"ב בסק"ט במה שכתב דהמברך עם הקטנים לא יצא י"ח. ואעפ"כ נ"ל דאם לא אכל כדי שביעה דאז חיוב בהמ"ז שלו הוא מדרבנן אפשר דיש לסמוך בדיעבד על דעת הרדב"ז שכמה מהאחרונים הסכימו לדבריו דבמצוה דרבנן אין צריך כונה לצאת ואין צריך לחזור ולברך ואף דהט"ז כתב דזה הוי כמכוין שלא לצאת והביא לזה ראיה מדברי הרא"ש תמוה דהרא"ש והרי"ף לשיטתייהו דס"ל בעלמא מצות צ"כ כמו שכתב הרא"ש בר"ה אבל למאן דסבירא ליה מצות א"צ כונה אימא ה"נ דיצא כמו תוקע להתלמד ובלא"ה ראייתו צע"ג כמו שהקשו עליו היד אפרים והא"ר עי"ש. ולכתחלה מי שיש עליו חיוב בהמ"ז ורוצה לברך עם קטנים לחנכם יתנהג בא' משתים או שיכוין לצאת בזה ג"כ עבור עצמו ויוצא בזה כמו שכתבנו במ"ב בשם הא"ר או שיכוין בפירוש שלא לצאת ויברך אח"כ עבור עצמו:

In order to fulfill performance. See *Mishnah Berurah*, sub-paragraph 9, where he writes that one who recites the Grace after meals with youngsters does not fulfill his obligation. Nevertheless, it seems to me that if he didn't eat to satiety—in which case his obligation to say Grace is Rabbinic in origin—then possibly after the fact one could rely on the opinion of the *Radvaz* with whose words many of the later authorities agree, that regarding a Rabbinic command there is no need for intent in order to fulfill one's obligation and there is no need to go back and repeat Grace. And even though the *Taz* writes that this act of leading the youngsters in Grace is equivalent to consciously intending not to fulfill one's obligation, and he brings proof for this from the words of the *Rosh*, his position is hard to understand, since the *Rosh* and the *Rif* are speaking in light of their own conviction in which they argue that mitzvos always require intent, as the *Rosh* writes in *Rosh Hashanah*. However, according to the one who says that mitzvos do not require intent it can be said here also that he has fulfilled the mitzvah, similar to one who blows the shofar to practice. Even without this, the Taz's proof requires more support in light of the questions raised by the *Yad Ephraim* and *Eliyahu Raba*; examine there.

Ideally, one who is obligated to say Grace and wishes to make the blessing together with youngsters in order to educate them should conduct himself in one of two ways. Either he should have intent to also fulfill his own obligation with this recitation, as we have written in *Mishnah Berurah* in the name of *Eliyahu Raba*; or, he should expressly intend not to fulfill his own obligation with this recitation, and then afterward repeat Grace to fulfill his own obligation.

APPENDIX II

Helpful Ideas for Putting This Book into Practice

This book has been divided into thirty daily segments so that the reader who so wishes can integrate the ideas presented here into his or her daily life on a manageable basis. Nevertheless, not every day will present opportunities to exercise the ideas expressed in the segment that was read that day. Even if such opportunity was present on the day of reading, it may require some practice before one automatically attunes one's mind to the desired consciousness. For this reason, the following paragraphs group reward mile opportunities by keywords that describe a common encounter or activity for the reader to focus upon to develop his conscious awareness.

The keywords are:

- Evening
- Morning
- Shul time
- Meal time
- Driving
- Working
- Shopping
- Socializing
- Dispensing money
- Volunteering

For each of these words or phrases, a listing follows that briefly describes the mitzvah activities that might occur that deserve more awareness, together with a reference to the page on which that mitzvah was discussed in more detail. In some cases, the word "website" appears instead of a page number. This is the case for new reward mile opportunities that were discovered as the contents of the book were developed and discussed, but came up too late to insert in the main body of the book. Accordingly, they are mentioned in this appendix with the intention of treating them more fully on the website rewardmilestoheaven.com, where users will be able to access this information, as well as add to it.

Evening

- When quizzing the children or reviewing homework, we should have in mind the part of the mitzvah of Transmit Torah that focuses on teaching Torah (p. 133).
- When opening and sorting the mail, keep in mind the mitzvos that you might encounter, such as:
    - "Give charity; don't be a tightwad" (p. 163) when recognizing and prioritizing solicitation letters;
    - "Make the payroll on time; don't delay" (p. 171) when scheduling the bills for timely payment; and
    - "Love your neighbor" (p. 23) when responding to simcha invitations.
- When attending a regular shiur or learning with a chavrusa, keep in mind the same mitzvah of Transmit Torah—this time the parts about learning (p. 124) and setting times (p. 129).
- When reviewing Torah learning, remember the part of the mitzvah of Transmit Torah that adjures us, "Don't forget" (p. 127); this would also apply when attending a community

event, such as a fundraiser, at which a speaker is trying to inspire us with ideas that we already know.

- Attending a simcha and cementing the bonds of friendship and community is certainly a time to be conscious of the deeper intent of the mitzvah, "Love your neighbor" (p. 23), but also be mindful of the mitzvah, "Love the stranger" (p. 81) when welcoming the "other side" of the family to your area.
- When paying the babysitter at the end of an evening out, remember the mitzvos, "Make the payroll on time; don't delay" (p. 171), and then, when showing the same concern for her as you would to a member of your own family by driving or escorting her home, remember the mitzvah of "Love your neighbor" (p. 23).
- On Shabbos or Yom Tov, when entering your dark bedroom and keeping the door open to get your bearings instead of turning on the light, remember that you are fulfilling the mitzvah to rest (cease labor) on Shabbos or Yom Tov.

Morning

- When waking early and treading quietly so as not to disturb others, remember the mitzvah of not robbing (see website).
- When reading the weekly parsha as the Sages have instructed—twice in the original, once in the translation—remember also that part of the mitzvah of Transmit Torah that adjures us, "Don't forget" (p. 127).
- During the morning rush, when properly criticizing a family member, remember the mitzvah, "Speak up and speak out" (p. 43).
- During the morning rush, when ignoring slight offenses, make yourself aware of the mitzvos to not embarrass (p. 61) and to not bear a grudge (p. 37), as appropriate.

- When coaching the children on making brachos, keep in mind the mitzvah of "Transmit Torah" (p. 121).
- While rushing to make it to work on time, keep in mind the mitzvah, "Don't take early lunch breaks" (p. 185).
- When reading the paper and taking particular interest in stories about Jews or affecting Jews, realize that you are experiencing a sense of community and remember the mitzvah, "Love your neighbor" (p. 23).
- During the same session, when skipping stories about wicked people, remember the mitzvah, "Do not favor evil people" (p. 95), and when ignoring horoscopes and similar articles, the mitzvah, "Don't read junk" (p. 141).

Shul Time

- While saying Shema, remember also the mitzvah of studying the Torah day and night as you contemplate the deeper meaning of the words (p. 129). Also have this in mind when learning in shul.
- While concentrating on a particular need during prayers, remember the mitzvah to "Just ask G-d" (p. 111).
- When saying *"hayom yom ..."* before the Psalm of the day, realize that this statement is a performance of the mitzvah, "Remember the Shabbos to make it holy" (see website).
- When greeting someone new in shul, making them feel welcome, finding them a seat or giving them an aliya, keep in mind the mitzvah of loving a stranger (p. 81).
- When clarifying a halacha with the Rav, remember the mitzvah to transmit Torah, especially the part about learning (p. 124).
- When shmoozing during permissible times with a learned member of the community, remember the mitzvah of holy alliances (p. 69).

- Any time you are alone with your thoughts and an old embarrassment pops into your mind that makes you cringe, remember the mitzvah, "Promise G-d" (p. 115), and the three-part formula for confessing mistakes.

Meal Time

- Whenever striving to eat a properly balanced meal, in order to provide the health and energy to fulfill mitzvos, remember the staying healthy part of the mitzvah, "Be Like G-d" (p. 103).
- When helping to serve, remember the mitzvah, "Give a lift" (p. 145).
- When controlling your appetite for whatever reason (e.g., diet, to leave over enough for others, to wait for the hostess to join or the host to start eating), realize that self-control is an expression of the mitzvah, "Be like G-d" (p. 103).
- When really enjoying a particular dish and enthusiastically recommending it to another, realize how much you wish to share the pleasure and that this is an expression of the mitzvah, "Love your neighbor" (p. 23).
- When singing Shabbos songs at the table, keep in mind that this is an example of the mitzvah, "Remember the Shabbos to make it holy" (see website).
- When quizzing the children in between courses, remember the teaching part (p. 133) of the mitzvah, "Transmit Torah."
- During discussions of family matters and preferences, it is sometimes necessary to correct the attitude or behavior of a family member. At such times, keep in mind the mitzvah of "Speak up and speak out" (p. 43) and its recommended tactics of speaking softly.

- When the decision is *not* to correct a family member, consider whether this is an instance of the mitzvah, "Do not embarrass people" (p. 61), or perhaps the mitzvah of "Do not bear a grudge" (p. 37), when one is simply ignoring and adjusting to another's bad habit.
- When shouting at another out of exasperation, at least remember the "don't resent silently" (p. 57) part of the mitzvah, "Do not hate your brother in your heart."
- When telling over a true but salacious story while purposely omitting names, be mindful of the mitzvah, "Don't speak harmfully" (see website).

Driving

- When picking up someone who needs a lift, either arranged (e.g., one's spouse at the airport) or not (e.g., an acquaintance at the bus stop), keep in mind the mitzvah, "Give a lift" (p. 145).
- When picking up a senior under any circumstances, also keep in mind the mitzvah, "Raise them high" (p. 85).
- After observing another car needing help and either helping directly or calling for help, remember the mitzvah, "Give a lift" (p. 145).
- At all times, while doing a car pool when it's not your turn, realize that you are fulfilling the mitzvah, "Love your neighbor" (p. 23).
- When listening to the radio and changing channels because you recognize opinion pieces contrary to Torah, remember the mitzvah, "Don't read junk" (p. 141).
- When asking or motioning to the car standing next to you to lower the volume on his blaring radio, remember the "*sinah* as resentment" (p. 57) part of the mitzvah, "Do not hate your brother in your heart."

- With regard to listening to Torah tapes—
  - Of course, remember the learning part (p. 124) of the mitzvah, "Transmit Torah";
  - Also, if this is a regular time such as driving to and from work, remember while inserting the tape the part of the mitzvah about setting times for Torah study (p. 129);
  - If you've already listened to that particular tape before, remember the part of the mitzvah about not forgetting (p. 127).
- When taking precaution to ensure that you drive safely in a safe vehicle, remember the staying healthy part of the mitzvah, "Be Like G-d" (p. 103).
- After experiencing the bad driving habits of others but managing to control your anger (e.g., not cutting them off in turn), remember that such self-control is an expression of the mitzvah, "Be like G-d" (p. 103); if the offending driver turns out to be someone you know and you decide to put it out of your mind, then also remember the mitzvah, "Do not bear a grudge" (p. 37).
- When "hoping" to find a parking spot, light traffic conditions, or a timely gas station, etc., be aware of the mitzvah, "Just ask G-d" (p. 111) (especially since it will also help you articulate the prayer in the proper manner).

Working

- When working with junior employees and "showing them the ropes," remember the mitzvah, "Love your neighbor" (p. 23).
- When working with senior employees and showing them deference, remember the mitzvah, "Raise them high" (p. 85).
- When showing new employees where to get coffee or how to fill out a time sheet, etc., remember the mitzvah, "Love the stranger" (p. 81).

- While listening to a troubled employee and expressing concern and understanding, remember that such compassion is part of the mitzvah, "Be like G-d" (p. 103).
- While filling out an expense claim and carefully recording and totaling the items, keep in mind the mitzvah, "Don't pad the expense account" (p. 189).
- When doing whatever it takes to be sure to return on time from lunch or a coffee break (e.g., keeping an eye on the wall clock, setting an alarm or just taking the minimum time necessary), remember the mitzvah, "Don't take early lunch breaks" (p. 185).
- In the process of negotiating a contract with a supplier or customer, remember the mitzvah, "Let's make a deal" (and especially the lessons it teaches—see p. 199).
- Whenever acting humbly, such as when denying the full credit that you really deserve, or when soliciting ideas from others even though you are satisfied with your own analysis, realize that such humility emulates the Almighty as expressed in the mitzvah, "Be like G-d" (p. 103).
- In addition, when working in a group and sharing the credit for a noticeable achievement, remember also the mitzvah, "Indulge the employees" (p. 179).
- If you manage kitchen help (professionally or at home) and let them taste the food they are preparing, remember that this is in concert with the mitzvah, "Indulge the employees" (p. 179).
- Should you find it necessary to criticize a colleague for poor performance, find resolve from the mitzvah, "Speak up and speak out" (p. 43), which also provides useful guidelines.
- On the other hand, if you decide to ignore a colleague's momentary lapse, remember the mitzvah, "Do not bear a grudge" (p. 37).

- Should you choose to work with someone you don't like, hoping to improve the relationship, even if it wasn't your first choice, realize that this is a sublime performance of the mitzvah, "Don't pass up an opportunity" (p. 151) and the "*sinah* as dislike" (p. 50) part of the mitzvah, "Do not hate your brother in your heart."
- When blurting out your dismay when someone lets you down, remember the "*sinah* as resentment" (p. 57) part of the mitzvah, "Do not hate your brother in your heart."
- When avoiding or minimizing social time with non-Jewish co-workers (e.g., at an office party), remember the details of the mitzvah, "Don't marry out" (p. 75).

Shopping

- When deliberately patronizing Jewish shops instead of getting a better deal at a national chain store, realize that such concern for the livelihood of a fellow Jew is a premium performance of the mitzvah, "Love your neighbor" (p. 23).
- When the person running the store is a Torah sage or his wife, then your experiences there could involve performing the mitzvah, "Holy alliances" (p. 69).
- When phoning your parents to see if they need anything from the store in which you are shopping (e.g., you see a good buy that you know they would appreciate), keep in mind the mitzvah, "Honor your parents" (see website).
- Also keep in mind the mitzvah of "Love your neighbor" (p. 23) when you are so enthused about a purchase that you want to buy extra for someone else, whether that someone else is your parents, spouse or good friend, because these are all instances of treating another as yourself.
- When paying for any service (e.g., cleaning, shoe repair,

taxi/bus, etc.), even though you may have little choice, realize that you are conforming to the social norms desired by the Almighty, as expressed through the mitzvos of "Make the payroll on time; Don't delay" (p. 171).

- When reviewing all the details of a big ticket item (e.g., a car or a computer system), such as the terms, warranty and the like, remember that this is in concert with the mitzvah of "Let's make a deal" (p. 199).
- Even on purchases of much less significance, keep in mind the details of the mitzvah, "Let's make a deal" (p. 199); for example, when paying and taking the items that you have asked the storeowner to wrap or bag for you.

Socializing

- When seeking opportunities to converse or listen to Torah sages, or even eavesdrop on their conversations, remember the mitzvah, "Holy alliances" (p. 69).
- While discussing common challenges (e.g., household management, child rearing, etc.) with family, friends or acquaintances, and sharing your solutions, remember the mitzvah, "Love your neighbor" (p. 23).
- At the occasion of a family reunion, you may learn of someone's financial difficulty and offer assistance because you remember from the details of the mitzvos, "Give charity; Don't be a tightwad" (p. 163) that the best allocation of charity funds is to those close to you.
- When pulling shy members into a group picture, remember the mitzvah, "Love the stranger" (p. 81).
- When dancing and rejoicing at a wedding, remember the mitzvah, "Love your neighbor" (p. 23).
- While trying to turn the discussion away from trivia

toward Torah issues, remember all the facets of the mitzvah, "Transmit Torah" (p. 121).

- Whenever you are acting courteously, listening to others, or just simply providing a friendly smile to all whom you greet, remember the mitzvah, "Love your neighbor" (p. 23).
- More importantly, when conversing with someone who is not really on your wavelength and you are desperately searching for common ground, remember the "*sinah* as dislike" (p. 50) part of the mitzvah, "Do not hate your brother in your heart."
- When refraining from showing up someone who is bragging or stretching the truth, remember the mitzvah, "Do not embarrass people" (p. 61).
- When encouraging non-religious relatives to relay their expectations of marrying Jewish to their children, remember the mitzvah, "Don't marry out" (p. 75).
- When arranging for a party (e.g., wedding, bar mitzvah, etc.) and including an allowance for the servers to eat, remember the mitzvah, "Indulge the employees" (p. 179).

Dispensing Money

- While calculating the payroll and/or signing the checks, remember the mitzvos, "Make the payroll on time; Don't delay" (p. 171).
- When paying promptly for services rendered (e.g., babysitter, cleaning, waiter, transportation, etc.), remember the mitzvos, "Make the payroll on time; Don't delay" (p. 171).
- When considering a charity solicitation and hearing the stories about the needy Torah scholar(s), remember the mitzvah, "Holy alliances" (p. 69).
- When scheduling the right date to pay for service bills that arrive in the mail, remember the mitzvos, "Make the payroll on time; Don't delay" (p. 171).

- When filling out the postdated checks for your children's tuition, remember the teaching part of the mitzvah, "Transmit Torah" (p. 133); do the same when paying their tutor, but also remember the mitzvos, "Make the payroll on time; Don't delay" (p. 171) if you are paying at the agreed-upon time.
- When calculating the household budget and separating a part for charity, remember the mitzvos, "Give charity; Don't be a tightwad" (p. 163).

Volunteering

- When working at any community organization (e.g., health care facility, school, chessed project), remember the mitzvah, "Love your neighbor" (p. 23).
- In addition, when helping a senior, remember the mitzvah, "Raise them high" (p. 85).
- When you decide to care for an injured animal (for example, by calling the ASPCA) or recognize a lost pet and notify the owner, remember the mitzvah, "Don't pass up an opportunity" (p. 151).
- When you accept to learn with a chavrusa who is weaker than you, remember the teaching part of the mitzvah of Transmit Torah (p. 133).
- When organizing or attending a rally to oppose a wrong-headed idea, remember the mitzvah, "Do not favor evil people" (p. 95); if the wrongdoer is a fellow Jew (G-d preserve us), remember also the "*sinah* as hate" (p. 55) part of the mitzvah, "Do not hate your brother in your heart."
- When volunteering the name of one Jewish single to another, remember the mitzvah, "Don't marry out" (p. 75), as you imply the importance of marrying Jewish—all the more true if you have volunteered to help organize a Jewish singles event.

APPENDIX III

The Mitzvah Misdeed

The goal of this book is to benefit people with more reward for the mitzvos that they already do. The mitzvah to wear tefillin presents a similar opportunity. Many people will not be rewarded for this mitzvah because they don't quite do it right.

Surprisingly, this is not a new problem. The *Aruch HaShulchan* in *Orech Chaim*, 27:20 describes many G-d-fearing Jews as never having worn tefillin in their lives because of this misplacement. He bemoans the retribution they will face for never having fulfilled the mitzvah and for, instead, having uttered the associated blessings in vain. He concludes by noting that some people take the trouble to try and correct their fellow Jews, and for this their reward is very great.

I have observed this problem in every shul I have visited, in many different communities, and in some yeshivas of the highest caliber. Part of the problem appears to be a lack of discussion. In my shul I made the following 30-second announcement before *Ashrei/Uva L'Tzion* and saw an immediate improvement: "Please be reminded that every *posek* says that the front of the tefillin on the head has to be behind the original hairline. If it is over that line, you are not wearing head tefillin. For many people, the front of the tefillin is floating in the air because of the curvature of the skull. If you rock it forward until the front edge touches your scalp, you can tell if it is too far forward. I have a leaflet that explains this in more detail." It's a good idea not to look at anyone in particular when making the announcement so that no one feels they are being singled out. Repeating this brief announcement intermittently and posting the leaflet could correct a problem that has plagued the Jewish people for generations!

The following page, which explains the problem and solution, is designed as an attention-grabbing one-page leaflet. If you enlarge it by 123%, it will fill a standard letter-sized page. Feel free to copy it and post it or hand it out wherever you feel appropriate.

Are Your Tefillin Suffering From Attention Deficit Disorder?

You may be wearing your tefillin wrong without realizing it.

The Problem Up Front: All authorities agree that the front edge of the head tefillin should not extend past the original hairline. *(Shulchan Aruch, Rama, Rav Shulchan Aruch, Mishnah Berurah, Aruch HaShulchan, Kaf HaChaim)* Unfortunately, our tefillin often do so when—because our heads curve at the hairline—the front of the tefillin juts into the air.

The Solution: The best way to see if the tefillin are in the right place is to rock them forward, on their axis, until the front edge of the tefillin is pressed down against the scalp. If roots of the hair are still visible in front of the edge, then it's good.

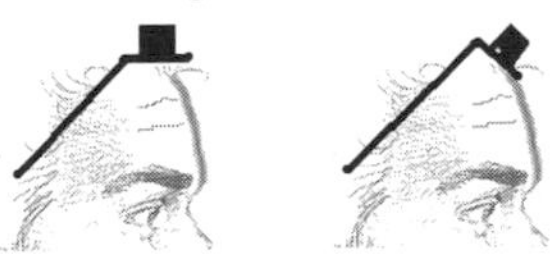

For people whose original hairline has receded, another indicator is necessary. If there is at least 2 fingerbreadths (*Sukkah* 5a, bottom *Tosfos*) of space between the top frown crease of the forehead and the pressed-down front edge, the tefillin are not too far forward.

It is not easy to determine yourself if your tefillin are properly placed. Better to ask someone (which will also publicize the issue). Don't hesitate to correct others lest you become guilty of not wearing head tefillin yourself, even though yours are perfectly placed. Sound strange? Read on!

Double Jeopardy: The mitzvah of *hocheach tochiach* instructs us to advise each other about any shortcomings whenever one person can have a positive influence on another. Surely, anyone wearing tefillin wants to fulfill the mitzvah. If you see someone wearing his tefillin too far forward and don't tell him, not only have you failed to perform the mitzvah of *tochachah*, Chazal tell us that you also must assume the failure for the tefillin not being worn! *In this way, you can wear tefillin properly and still be counted as not having done so.*

Look Forward, Not Back: If you find that you have been wearing your tefillin too low, *please* do not feel bad, and certainly don't hesitate to change because of a lifelong habit. Instead, realize the opportunity to perform *teshuvah in its highest form*. Precisely because it is not easy to change a lifelong habit, Chazal described a *baal teshuvah* as standing higher than the greatest tzaddik.

Keep It Up: The new position will feel strange for awhile. You may even have to move the knot because the straps have stretched over the years. View it as a small price to pay to know that you are doing better now.

Sources: See *Mishnah Berurah* 27:33, especially toward the end, where he suggests that the tefillin be worn even a little higher than this so that they don't slip over the line. See also *Aruch HaShulchan* 27:20, where he bemoans the fate of the many *frum* Jews who wear their tefillin too far forward, and so have never fulfilled the mitzvah properly in their lives!

ABOUT THE AUTHOR

Rabbi Shlomo Schwartz's penchant for infusing Torah values into everyday life is based on a lifetime of training and trying. From early on his education combined rigorous courses in both Torah and secular studies at Eitz Chaim Day Schools and Ner Israel Yeshiva College of Toronto. While pursuing *semicha* in the Bais Medrash Program of Ner Israel, he simultaneously achieved a B.A. (Psychology) through the evening program at the University of Toronto. Later, he did the same while serving as teacher and principal of Vancouver Talmud Torah, securing an M.A. (Education) from Simon Fraser University.

Rabbi Schwartz has integrated Torah living into a wide range of careers. After having been a day school teacher and principal, he followed with careers as a Chartered Accountant, Software Engineer, Documentation Writer, Comptroller, and Property Manager, all the while maintaining voluntary roles as Rabbi and teacher with various institutions such as Congregation Shaarei Tzedek (Windsor), Bnai Torah Youth Program (Toronto), Aish HaTorah (Thornhill and Discovery Program), NCSY (Ontario Region) and Shomer Israel Congregation (Toronto).

Rabbi Schwartz's goals for Torah living have been markedly inspired by his close ties with a number of world-changing personalities such as Rosh Yeshiva Rav Yaakov Weinberg, *zt"l*, Rav Noach Weinberg, Rav Chaim Mintz, Rav Sholom Gold, Rav Pinchas Lipner, Rav Nota Schiller, Rav Yissocher Frand and Rav Akiva Greenberg.

Rabbi Schwartz has lectured at synagogues, kollels, high schools, universities and adult education groups across Canada and the US.

You can visit the author's website at www.rewardmilestoheaven.com.